7·31·16

Eileen –
You are a gift.
God Bless and

Stay On Fire!

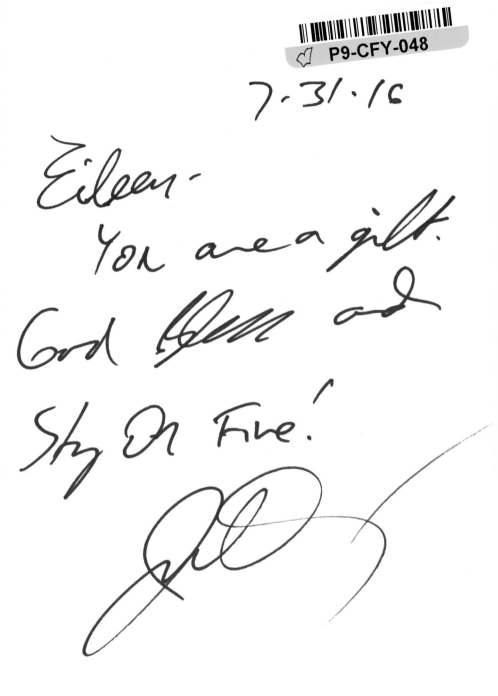

NORTH
STAR
WAY

ON FIRE

The 7 Choices to Ignite a Radically Inspired Life

JOHN O'LEARY

with Cynthia DiTiberio

NORTH STAR WAY

New York   London   Toronto   Sydney   New Delhi

North Star Way
An Imprint of Simon & Schuster, Inc.
1230 Avenue of the Americas
New York, NY 10020

First North Star Way hardcover edition March 2016

NORTH STAR WAY and colophon are registered trademarks of Simon & Schuster, Inc.

For information about special discounts for bulk purchases, please contact Simon & Schuster Special Sales at 1-866-506-1949 or business@simonandschuster.com.

The North Star Way Speakers Bureau can bring authors to your live event. For more information or to book an event contact the North Star Way Speakers Bureau at 1-212-698-8888 or visit our website at www.thenorthstarway.com.

Interior design by Jaime Putorti

Photo on p. 270 by SPG Photography, Susie Gaal

Manufactured in the United States of America

10 9 8 7 6 5 4 3 2

Library of Congress Cataloging-in-Publication Data

O'Leary, John–author.
  On fire : the 7 choices to ignite a radically inspired life / John O'Leary.
    pages cm
1. Conduct of life. 2. Self-realization. I. Title.
  BJ1589.O44 2016
  158.1—dc23
                              2015027012

ISBN 978-1-5011-1772-5
ISBN 978-1-5011-1774-9 (ebook)

To my wife, Beth.

The night we met, you had the courage to take my hand and dance. We've danced together through friendship, dating, marriage, parenting, challenges, joys, and life ever since. Thank you for being a constant encouragement, a wonderful mother, an awesome wife, and my best friend.

I love you.

CONTENTS

CONTENTS

ABLAZE

*The most powerful weapon on earth is
the human soul on fire.*
—*Marshal Ferdinand Foch*

$Y_{es.}$

It was a simple answer.

And it wasn't the one he was expecting.

I was standing in the front of a crowded auditorium in Shanghai and had just finished sharing the defining story of my life. For the previous hour during my keynote speech I'd described the day I was terribly burned as a child, the months I spent in the hospital, and the vast challenges I faced afterward.

It was a devastating, transformative, and tragic experience.

So this man asked a question with a seemingly obvious answer:

"John, if you could go back in time, go back to that Saturday morning, go back to that moment when you picked up the gasoline and got burned, would you do it all again?"

I looked at him, thought about it for a moment, and answered honestly.

Yes!

He looked at me with a puzzled expression.

Would you really choose to almost die? Would you choose to be burned on 100 percent of your body? Would you actually opt in to the desperate fight for life, or spending five months in the hospital, or being barely functioning for another eight months after that? And would you seriously choose to walk through life with scars covering your body, fingers amputated, and whispered glances and pointed fingers every day of your life?

Yes!

And I'll tell you why.

The fire was devastating, almost killed me, and certainly sparked a lifetime of challenges.

But it also molded me into who I am today.

So while it is true that if I'd not been burned, I'd remove all the difficulties caused by the fire. It is also true that I'd destroy all the gifts galvanized because of it.

You see, everything beautiful and enriching in my life today was born through the tragedy of those flames. Through the painful ashes of recovery as a child, I grew in character, audacity, compassion, faithfulness, and drive. It led to a clear perspective on what actually matters and a bold vision for what's possible.

Because of the fire, I don't take things for granted, am grateful for each day, and am certain that the best is yet to come.

The fire matured my grade-school community. It transformed little kids into compassionate, helpful classmates willing to serve their fellow student who now had some special needs. It later guided the decisions on where I went to high school and to university, which led to a fortuitous meeting with a beautiful lady named Beth, which led to four little kids.

Today I live an awesome life; a radically inspired life.

A *radically inspired life* means you embrace the lessons from your past, actively engage in the miracle of each moment, and ignite the limitless possibility of tomorrow. Now, it certainly doesn't mean a painless existence of error-free living. Far from it. But a radically inspired life means you possess the ability to learn from past mistakes, rise above personal challenges, and thrive in life, no matter your circumstances.

I wouldn't be living a radically inspired life had I not been burned in that fire.

Do I have scars?

You bet. They cover my entire body.

Did I lose my fingers?

Yes.

Was it devastating for my family?

Undoubtedly.

But we overcame.

It no longer negatively defines us.

In fact, we're significantly better because of it.

And we're not alone.

We all face fires in life, we all get burned.

We all endure moments when everything in life seems to be progressing exactly as planned: our kids are healthy, business is thriving, and dreams are unfolding, and then *boom!* An explosion.

Life completely changes.

Maybe your moment was an unwanted diagnosis.

A sick child.

A sudden death.

A business deal gone bad.

Regardless of the cause, your entire life was rocked.

I call these moments *inflection points*. This is a pinpointed moment in time that changes everything that follows. In an instant, the trajectories of life, business, and relationships are altered.

There are positive scenarios, too.

The moment a new relationship buds, the offer of an incredible opportunity at work, or coming to a new understanding or perspective in life.

More important than the inflection point itself is how you choose to react to it. Whether that moment ends up impacting your life positively or negatively is, ultimately, a choice.

It's your choice.

These choices add up to the life you are living today.

And these choices determine the life you'll lead tomorrow.

I write this book to wake you up to the reality that you have one life to live, one opportunity to impact, and one legacy to author. Whether your life story is an epic to celebrate or a trag-edy to mourn has little to do with the events within your life and everything to do with the manner in which you respond to those events. From now on, no more sleepwalking; no more accidental living.

This book will remind you that you can't always choose the path that you walk in life, but you can always choose the manner in which you walk it.

It will inspire you to harness the power of your daily choices, the worthiness of your personal story, and the strength of your inner purpose.

It will free you to respond *Yes* to past adversity, *Yes* to future possibility, and *Yes* to waking up to the miraculous gift of each moment.

And it will ignite you to be absolutely *On Fire* for your life.

———

So, would I do it again?

Yes!

And as you read on, you'll know why and agree that you would, too.

Set before you are fire and water.

To whatever you choose, stretch out your hand.

Before everyone are life and death.

Whichever they choose will be given them.

—SIRACH, 200 BC

1

DO YOU WANT TO DIE?

Life is not about avoiding death;
it's about choosing to really live.

*T*he nurses seem frantic.

They keep telling me everything is okay. That I'm going to be fine. They say they'll stay with me and there is nothing to worry about.

So why are they racing around me?

Why do they seem panicked?

Why do they continue to poke me and stick me and whisper about me?

I watch them buzzing around me.

Then I look down at my body; it doesn't look like me.

I look at my hands, but they don't look like my hands. I look at the remnants of my green sweat suit and tennis shoes; they've become one with my arms and legs.

The pain is intense.

The fire this morning changed everything.

Everything.

A nurse says again that it's going to be okay. I know she's wrong.

I really messed up today. Today, I blew up my parents' garage.

I didn't mean to.

It wasn't even my fault, really.

It's just that earlier this week, I watched some older kids in my neighborhood playing with fire. They dripped a little gasoline on the sidewalk, stood back, and then one of the big kids from seventh grade threw a match on top.

The puddle sparked to life.

It was amazing!

I figured if they could do it and get away with it, so could I.

So this morning, with Mom and Dad out of the house, I went into the garage. I lit a small piece of cardboard on fire, walked over to the five-gallon barrel of gasoline, and tilted it to pour a little gasoline on the piece of cardboard.

Just like the older boys, I wanted to make the flame dance.

But the big red barrel was too heavy to lift.

So I set the burning piece of cardboard on the concrete garage floor.

I knelt down, bear-hugged the can, and carefully tilted it toward the flame.

I waited for the liquid to come out.

It never did.

What I remember next was a big boom. The explosion launched me against the wall on the far side of the garage.

My ears rang.

My body hurt.

My clothes were drenched in gasoline.

I was on fire.

I was on fire!

I felt dizzy. Everything around me was ablaze. The only way I could get out of the garage was to go back through the flames.

Yes, I remembered being taught to stop-drop-and-roll.

But I was so scared.

I was in so much pain.

I needed someone to save me.

So I just ran.

I ran through the flames.

I ran up two steps and opened the door to the house. I ran struggling and screaming into the house. Running around downstairs, not sure what else to do. Yelling for someone, anyone, to help me.

I stood in the front hall, screaming.

I was still on fire.

Two of my sisters came down the stairs. They looked at me, covered their faces, and screamed in horror.

Then I saw my older brother, Jim. He raced toward me. He picked up our front doormat and started hitting me with it. He just kept swinging that mat into me. Then he tackled me to the ground, wrapped me in the rug, and carried me outside.

The fire was out.

But the damage was done.

A few minutes later the ambulance came hurtling down the street.

I tried to run to it, but my legs would barely move. So I hobbled. Naked. My skin and clothes had been burned off.

I was so hoping no one would see me.

I was embarrassed. I was scared. I was cold.

I just wanted to get inside.

I climbed in the ambulance and Jim was right behind me, ready to hop in. "Sorry, you can't come," the paramedic said as he shut one of the doors.

Jim tried to argue with him, he explained we were brothers, but the man just said, "I am sorry." And pulled the other door shut.

The ambulance pulled away. Through the back window I watched my brother and two sisters standing in the front yard, smoke rising behind them.

We drove away.

That all happened this morning.

Now I'm here in some emergency room.

Everything has changed.

I feel desperately alone.

And then, I hear a voice in the hallway.

Mom!

Finally!

She always makes everything better. I know she can fix this.

I hear her footsteps.

I see the curtain surrounding me pulled back.

She comes right over to my side, takes my burned hand in hers, gently pats my bald, raw head.

"Hi, baby," she says, a smile on her face.

I look at my mom. Tears that I didn't even realize I was holding back begin falling down my cheeks. "Mommy," I say, my voice shaking in fear. "Am I going to die?"

I know it's bad. And I so much want her warm encouragement. I want her to brush my fears away. I want to be cuddled and comforted with hope and reassurance. I want her to kiss it all away as only Mom can.

I wait for the promise that she'll take care of everything. She always does.

She always does.

Mom clasps my hand gently in hers.

She looks into my eyes.

Gathers her thoughts.

And asks, "John, do you want to die? It's your choice, not mine."

Three summers before the fire I was at a neighborhood swimming pool.

It was the kind of Midwest, July afternoon perfect for swimming. High humidity. Brutal heat. Blazing sun. Absolutely perfect!

The water was packed with kids and the deck jammed with parents. I was a couple of weeks from turning seven, was just learning how to swim, and loved my newfound independence. That's right, no more floaties for me!

But overconfidence can be deadly.

It caused me to get too close to the deep-end edge. My head was bobbing just above water as I bounced along the bottom of the pool, and then all of a sudden, I slid as if I were on ice. The gentle-sloping floor dropped off rapidly into the deep end of the pool. Nothing was underneath my feet. I lost my footing. I was sinking.

I slid all the way to the bottom. I didn't even try to move my arms or kick my legs. I'm not sure if I knew it was hopeless to try or if I knew someone would come for me. But I just sat there on the bottom of the pool.

Looking up.

Waiting.

Hoping.

Expecting.

Knowing.

Then the water broke open above me and a person quickly grabbed me, brought me to the surface, pulled me to the side of the pool, and I was out of the water. I looked up to see my savior, squinting my eyes in the sun.

It was my mom.

She'd jumped in fully clothed and pulled me out of the water.

She saved my life that day.

She just dried me off, wrapped herself with the towel, got me a Popsicle, took off her waterlogged watch, and moved on. She showed me that day and on innumerable other occasions she would be there for me. She would save me. I just had to reach out my hand to her.

So on the day I was burned, as she held my hand, and I asked if I was going to be okay, I already knew what she would do and the words she would speak.

"Baby, you are fine. We'll get you home today. If you are brave I'll get you a milk shake on the way home. All you need to think about right now is if you want chocolate or vanilla."

I wanted the milk shake promise!

Instead, I got this: "John, do you want to die? It's your choice, not mine."

Hold up. WHAT?

What kind of question is that to ask a scared little boy in an emergency room!?

SINK OR SWIM

You may be thinking that my mom was the coldest, most callous parent of all time.

I'm not going to argue with you on that point.

I mean, who doesn't offer his or her little boy, dying in a hospital bed, some love and encouragement? What kind of woman could be so absolutely indifferent and standoffish? Didn't she know that this poor little fella just *wanted* a little hope?

But what was it that I *needed*?

Because in retrospect, that was exactly what she delivered.

I remember looking up at her and responding, "I do not want to die. I want to live."

She answered, "Then, John, you need to fight like you've never fought before. You need to take the hand of God, and you need to walk this journey with Him. Race forward with everything you have. Daddy and I will be with you every step of the way. But, John, you listen to me: you need to fight for it."

You need to *fight* for it.

Before that day, I was a typical nine-year-old kid. I shirked responsibility and seldom owned my actions, and even less frequently the resulting effects. I cleaned my room because I had to. I did homework because they made me. I went to church because they told me to.

My parents were in charge.

I followed.

They gave me everything I needed and I happily accepted all of it. I was a bit . . . entitled.

I was the fourth born to parents who loved one another. They also adored all six of their kids.

I lived in a beautiful house.

I had a father who worked, a mother who stayed home.

I lived in a safe neighborhood.

Went to a great school.

We had church on Sundays, blueberry pancakes afterward, and fried chicken at Grandma's in the evening.

We even owned a golden retriever.

We had it all.

Life was perfect.

And then life changed.

It always does.

When life changes in this way, we can beg and plead to go back to the way things were. Feeling entitled to that reality. Waiting for someone to wave the magic wand and put things back to normal; back to the way life was.

Or we can step up, recognize that it is time to move forward from here, and embrace total accountability and ownership over our lives.

Own your life, John.

Fight for it.

It's your choice.

Not mine.

Mom's response demanded ownership. No more entitlement, no more shirking responsibility. She gave me truth.

Reflecting on it today, I see Mom's question was an *inflection point*—a moment in time that changes everything that follows.

That day, when it mattered most, I was teetering on the brink of death. Mom courageously walked to the edge of the cliff and looked over it with me. It wouldn't take much for me to give up, let go, and fall down into the abyss.

But there was an alternative path, a way forward. She pointed away from the cliff. In the other direction was a huge mountain. It looked impossible to climb. But she said that I could do it.

That I could choose to turn away from the edge and take small, shuffling steps, up the hill, back to life.

We all have that choice. We choose to vibrantly go about life, soak it up, embrace it, and celebrate it, or we choose not to. No one else can make this decision for us.

We get one life.

We either choose to live.

Or we choose to die.

DO YOU WANT TO DIE?

By all accounts, I should not have survived the fire.

After enduring several minutes engulfed in flames, I was burned on essentially 100 percent of my body.

Eighty-seven percent of my burns were third-degree.

The worst kind.

These burns were deep. They seared through the three layers of skin, through the muscle, and even all the way to the bone in places.

Burned skin will never grow back without donor skin. And, ironically, donor skin must come from the recipient's body. Since all of my skin was burned, the only donor site that could be harvested was from the least badly burned part of my body, my scalp. It was a near impossible task.

In addition, my lungs were damaged by smoke inhalation.

Controlling the core temperature of my body was difficult with no skin. Infections were likely.

Things were extraordinarily dire.

Today the mortality rate for burn patients is calculated by taking the percentage of the body burned and adding the age of the patient. So for me, almost three decades before many advances in burn treatment, the math worked like this: 100 percent of the body burned plus nine years of age equals absolutely no chance of survival.

The fire was a death sentence.

My mom didn't know all of this when she walked into the hospital room that morning. She didn't know much about how the fire started, what burn treatment consisted of, or what was to come next.

She didn't know at that moment the coming agony of going to bed nightly wondering if her little boy would be alive when the next day arrived. She never imagined pacing the hospital floors at night, crying in lonely, darkened corners of the halls, or enduring the hours of agonized waiting through dozens of surgeries with her son's life hanging in the balance.

All she knew—all we knew—was the fight was on.

Now, I feel obligated to tell you a secret and share some good news before we go on.

Spoiler alert: Don't read the next sentence if you want to be surprised by the end of the book.

The boy lives.

Yep, while those moments I described in the hospital are heartbreaking, every parent's worst nightmare, this book has a happy ending. Obviously, or you wouldn't be reading these words!

But it wasn't by accident.

I believe in the power of prayer. And I know thousands of prayers were offered up for me that night, and every day for the next five months I spent in the hospital. But I also believe that prayer is not so much intended to change God, but to inform and inspire the next steps of the individuals offering the prayer.

I survived because of the actions and encouragement of remarkable people by my side every step of the way, pushing me to fight, imploring me to believe, and empowering me to take ownership of my life.

And the little boy expected to die is now abundantly alive.

Today, I've been happily married for twelve years. My wife, Beth, and I have a strong marriage and four healthy, beautiful, and frequently rambunctious kids. Three boys and a girl. We live in an idyllic community, belong to an active church, and enjoy amazing lives.

This incredible life is the outgrowth of a daring question:

Do you want to die?

A bold question that reminds us that we hold the power to choose our path forward. We may not control everything that happens to us, but we always control how we respond.

Obviously my rash decision to play with fire was a huge inflection point.

I made a simple choice as a child. And in a moment my life, and the life of my family, would never be the same. There was no going back.

But that wasn't the only inflection point we faced. Countless others came in its wake. Moments in time that changed everything afterward. The choices we made would lead either to a life of hope and possibility or a life of fear and regret.

We all make these choices throughout our lives.

I hope to open your eyes, to help you truly see which path you are choosing to go down. And to point you toward the one filled with possibility.

The first choice you must make to ignite a radically inspired life is to _own_ your life. It is to leave entitlement behind and realize that it is up to _you_ to make the changes in your life.

Stop making excuses.

This is _your_ life.

Do you want to die?

No?

Good.

Then act like it.

NO MORE ACCIDENTS

One of my favorite movies is _Good Will Hunting_.

There's a powerful scene where a seemingly brash, arrogant, know-it-all young man is in the midst of a deep conversation with his psychologist about his past. Eventually, the psychologist tells the troubled young man:

It's not your fault.

It's not your fault.

It's not your fault!

This compelling scene is a pivotal moment in the movie. Embracing the freeing truth in those words would greatly benefit many of us in our lives.

Yet, my encouragement to you is quite different.

When my family and I recall the fire that changed our lives, we describe it as "John's accident" or simply "the accident." The term *accident* appears more than a dozen times in a book my mom and dad wrote about it called *Overwhelming Odds*.

Accident.

Let me ask you a question: What do you think happens when someone holds a flame to a can of gasoline?

Yup.

That's not an accident: it's a law of nature. It's the result of holding a burning object to highly combustible fumes.

Yes, I was a child.

Yes, I had no idea what would happen.

And, yes, I certainly didn't expect the massive explosion that took place, but to call it an accident cheapens my role in the event.

When my mom encouraged me that it was my choice whether I lived, she was doing something vitally important. She was challenging me to take full responsibility not only for what happened, but more important, for what would happen next. This was a defining inflection point for me. I had two choices . . . take responsibility for my healing and fight forward, or believe someone else would save me and passively endure.

My mom knew that this was life and death, that I was on the edge of a cliff. That if I didn't take the reins, I would fall into it and slip away. She knew that she could not make me do it. She understood that I needed to be accountable.

Accountability gets a bad rap these days. What do you think of when you think about accountability? Maybe you think of responsibilities, burdens, a weight you have to carry. Maybe you think of corporations that avoided accountability, that destroyed people's lives and shrugged their shoulders afterward.

Unfortunately at times it feels like we live in a society that loves to shirk responsibility and expects others to swoop in and save the day.

Ah, but accountability not only keeps you from accidentally slipping backwards in life, it frees you to intentionally navigate the path forward. It gives you the power to take ownership of your life.

STOP SHRUGGING

Personal accountability is a prerequisite for any worthy achievement.

Several years ago I was fortunate to be asked to give an inspirational speech about how to rise above challenges in the real estate market to the Staubach Company, a real estate company started by former naval officer and great Dallas Cowboys quarterback Roger Staubach. Over the following three decades it became hugely successful before Roger sold it for more than $600 million in 2008.

I flew to Dallas to speak to a gathering of their senior-level leaders. When my taxicab pulled up to their headquarters, the young woman who'd organized the event greeted me at the door. I smiled and we chatted as we walked to the room where I would prepare before going onstage.

Although I had researched the background of the company and spoken to several of the event's organizers, I thought I would take this chance to ask this woman what she felt was most critical to the company's long-standing success.

She paused as she poured me a cup of coffee.

She handed it to me.

And then said, "Well, there is this story that has become legend around here."

She explained how Roger Staubach had famously demanded accountability from every employee at the firm. He had learned the importance of accountability as a naval officer, seen its value repeatedly on the football field, and knew it was essential to grow a business and a life.

She explained that he empowered each employee to run his or her own business, support one another, and to responsibly work through any issues that arose, both with clients and within his or her team.

It didn't always go so smoothly.

One day two brokers approached Staubach unable to solve how to split a $16,000 commission. Each agent argued that the entire commission belonged to him. They'd been stuck in this argument for several days and finally went to their boss, threw up their hands, and said, "We can't solve this. Can you fix this for us?"

Staubach asked a few questions.

Thanked the two brokers for sharing.

He asked if they could see any way past their grievances, see the other's perspective and own a mutually beneficial outcome. They could not.

He asked if they would be willing to split the commission, recognizing that they both had done substantial work in securing the deal. They would not.

Staubach stood. He shook both their hands, thanked them for their work, and thanked them for their generosity.

He then legendarily took the entire commission and donated it to charity.

He wanted to let those brokers know that they would either be responsible for succeeding together, or be responsible for failing together. It was their choice.

No one else ever took such a complaint to the boss. Future problems were tackled as they occurred at the individuals' level.

I thanked the woman for sharing that story. It helped me understand the culture of that company and what kind of leadership advice might be relevant. But that story extends well beyond business.

Can you think of a time when you were tempted to be like those brokers?

Have you at times in your life wanted to shrug your shoulders, throw up your hands, and look for someone else to solve your problems? It's understandable to want to look outside yourself, to put the onus on other things or other people.

We frequently blame things outside of our control.

We point to situations: *It's not my fault. Traffic was bad. The markets stink. The world's a mess.*

We point to others: *It's not my fault. She is too difficult. My employees are idiots. My patients are needy. The commission is all mine.*

But excuses get you nowhere.

Here's my challenge: erase "It's not my fault" from your vocabulary. Every time you feel it coming to the surface, about to roll off your tongue—stop. Say instead, "It's my life and I'm responsible for it."

This changes everything.

It's my life and I'm responsible for it.

No one's going to save you.

Accountability means you take ownership of your own life. Realize that you hold the keys to changing things, solving your problems, improving your life, and making a difference. And it's not just about action and fixing. Accountability also provides the power to let things go, to surrender things you can't change, to forgive events and people that have burned you in the past. It demands that we stop shrugging our shoulders, throwing up our hands, thinking that we can do nothing.

Your life provides the daily inflection points to stop looking outside yourself, to stop waiting for someone else to change, and to stop passively waiting for someone else to step forward.

This is your moment to choose to live.

To really live.

Own it.

PICK UP YOUR FORK

Have you ever experienced the joy of feeling that you finally made it?

Perhaps it was graduating school, landing your first job, or getting married. You worked, strove, labored, and achieved. You summited a mighty peak—and then discovered that the difficult part of your journey was just beginning?

For me that experience was coming home after being burned. I was nine years old, had just spent almost five months in the hospital, endured a couple of dozen surgeries, and lost my fingers to amputation. The painful experience of being away from family, facing continuous procedures, was finally over. The struggle was over; the celebration was on!

The hospital that had admitted me with no chance of surviving was now releasing me back to my family. I was now burned, scarred, bandaged, and wheelchair bound, but very much alive and grateful.

We pulled out of the parking lot, made the five-minute drive home, and turned onto our street. I was absolutely overwhelmed by the cars, fire trucks, balloons, and friends lining our subdivision.

Under an awning, a line formed of family, friends, classmates, neighbors, first responders, and community members welcoming us home. Music played and people cried.

The miracle had happened.

The boy lived.

Eventually, though, our friends went home, the cars pulled away, the front door shut, and we were left to decide how we'd move forward as a family.

That night Mom made my favorite meal: au gratin potatoes. (If you hadn't figured it out yet, this likely just cemented it for you: I was a strange kid!) We sat around the kitchen table in our reconstructed house as a family for the first time since the night before the fire.

Dad and Mom sat at opposite ends of the table. Three of my sisters, Laura, Cadey, and Susan, lined one side, with my brother, Jim, my sister Amy, and me on the other. Our family had been through inconceivable trials over the preceding months.

We'd lost our house in the fire.

My siblings had lost their parents to their near-24/7 hospital vigil.

My brother and sisters, ranging in age from eighteen months to seventeen years old, had been split up, staying with friends and relatives until the house was rebuilt.

My parents almost lost their son.

I'd lost my fingers, the ability to walk, and was scarred from my neck to my toes.

And yet here we were.

We made it.

Home.

Together.

One family.

Changed.

Scarred.

Transformed.

And alive.

We were back to eating dinner, cleaning up spilled milk and worrying about elbows on the table. Life would return to normal. But undoubtedly, a miracle had occurred. So tonight we celebrated.

The food looked delicious. I closed my eyes and smelled the cheesy goodness. Then opened them and realized . . . I couldn't eat anything. Because of wrappings, splints, and my inability to hold a fork, I could not partake in my celebration meal. I stared at my plate, not sure what to do.

My sister Amy saw me struggling. So she thoughtfully grabbed my fork, speared a few potatoes, and elevated them toward my mouth.

Then I heard it.

"Put that fork down, Amy. If John is hungry, he'll feed himself."

I turned my head toward my mom.

What did she just say?

Put that fork down?

He'll feed himself?

What the heck, Mom? Haven't I already been through enough? Are you kidding me? I'm hungry and I can't eat!

That night I cried at the table. I got mad at my mom. I told her I could not do it, that it wasn't fair, and I'd been through enough. The night quickly shifted from celebration and laughter to upheaval and contention.

The party was over.

Mom ruined it all.

Yet that night also created another inflection point for a nine-year-old boy. As my siblings cleared their plates and my hunger and anger mounted, I wedged the fork between what remained of my two hands. My fingers had been amputated just above the bottom knuckles. Because the skin had still not entirely healed, my hands were wrapped in thick gauze. I looked like a boxer, fighting to get a fork between two boxing gloves.

It was painstakingly slow.

The fork repeatedly fell out of my grasp.

But eventually, I awkwardly stabbed at the potatoes, brought them to my mouth, and chewed them.

And stared angrily at my mom.

I was mad.

My hands throbbed.

She'd ruined my night.

I hated her.

But I was eating.

Looking back on it, I see what a courageous stand my Mom took. It must have been extremely painful for her to sit with the entire family watching her little guy. How much easier and seemingly more loving it would have been to just feed me those darn potatoes and bring out the ice-cream cake.

How much easier it is in life to not do—or to make others do—the hard stuff.

Easier to take a picture of the family with everybody smiling at the dinner table, a little kid in a wheelchair at the end, post on Facebook, and write, "Back to normal! We're all home and doing great!"

Mom wasn't worried about what others thought.

She wasn't concerned about Photoshopping the moment.

Mom utilized this moment as a reminder that others would be there to encourage, to serve, to love me. But this was still my fight, this was still my life. It might be ripe with challenges, but it was also my opportunity to realize that none of those obstacles would be insurmountable.

This moment was just the beginning of many times when I would have to find a way. She forced me to pick up my fork. And I'm completely convinced I would not be living the life I am today if she hadn't.

The day I was burned, she challenged me to choose not to die.

The night I came home, she freed me to choose to really live.

ENTITLEMENT V. OWNING IT

But until a person can say deeply and honestly, "I am what I am today because of the choices I made yesterday," that person cannot say, "I choose otherwise."
—Stephen Covey

Are you truly alive?

No.

I didn't just ask, "Are you breathing?"

I'm not asking if you have a pulse or are existing or enduring.

No, I want to know if you are really living.

Do you feel excited about your life? Like you are present for each moment, big and small? Like you can handle the challenges that come, embrace the opportunities before you, and be fully satisfied in any situation?

Are you living a radically inspired life?

If not, it's time to discover the power of taking ownership of your life. Regardless of the challenges you face today, this is a choice. A choice that ignites within us the power to surrender to things we just can't change, fight for the things we can, and celebrate each moment on the journey going forward.

Life is not about avoiding death, it's about choosing to really live.

Here is your inflection point.

No more *It's not my fault.*

Embrace the freedom of *It's my life.*

Because this is your life.

This is your time.

This is your moment.

This matters.

Act like it.

Choose to own it.

In our own woundedness,
we can become sources of life for others.

—HENRI J. M. NOUWEN

2

WHAT ARE YOU HIDING?

Stop pretending and begin to see the
miracle of your life.

*H*ere we go again.

I used to love taking a bath.

Now it's the worst part of my day.

Every morning two nurses pick me up out of bed, put me on a table with wheels, and push me down a long hallway and into a smelly, hot room with a big steel bathtub in the middle.

They pick me up off the table and slowly put me in the water.

My entire body is covered in these thick bandages. Below them are gauze pads. And below them is the big, red, open sore that used to be my body.

Everywhere the water touches . . . hurts.

Every time they try to peel off a bandage . . . it hurts.

Every time they scrub a wound . . . it hurts.

And because my whole body is without skin . . . it all hurts.

They tell me it's absolutely necessary. They tell me it's the only way to keep me safe. They tell me they do this to keep me alive.

Okay. Fine. Do it. But I still hate it.

When they're done cleaning me, they shave my head.

This is by far the worst.

They tell me the only donor site for skin grafts is my scalp. That means the doctors have to take a thin layer of skin from my head and put it on the parts of my body that don't have any skin. The nurses say hair is dirty and oily and might allow bacteria to grow. So they need to shave my head.

They do it every day.

It takes a few minutes, but it feels like a few hours.

They shave the same freaking place where they just took a piece of skin.

Finally, once they're done shaving and done cleaning, they take me out of the tub. They put me back on the cold metal table.

I'm cold. I'm naked. I'm scared. And I'm not done.

After they dry me off, they put on this white medicine called Silvadene. It looks like soft-serve vanilla ice cream. It goes on like sunscreen. And burns like heck. They rub it on every inch of my body.

Then they wrap me up like a big white mummy. Bandages cover my entire body. The whole process takes two hours.

They've been doing this for weeks.

But today, in this room, all the physical pain was nothing compared with what just sank in.

As I watch them pull off my bandages and uncover my body, I finally look at what is under all that gauze. Like, what is really underneath all that gauze.

The fire burned off all my skin.

It's all gone.

All that's left is the stuff beneath it. My hands, arms, legs, chest, stomach—all of me—is a red, open, ugly mess.

Seeing that, really seeing it, makes me sick to my stomach. I finally realize that I'll never be who I was. I'll never look the way I looked.

Then I realize something worse.

Something that causes even greater pain: not just my body is burned, but my face, too. My face must make me look like a big, red sore monster.

My life is over.

As they finish wrapping me, I can't even tell anyone. I can't talk because there is a hole in my neck. They call it a trach. It helps my lungs breathe. But it means I can't talk. I can't use my voice.

So I just cry.

When the nurses push me back to my room, Mom sees the tears rolling down my cheeks.

"Baby, what is it? Are you in pain? Do you need more painkillers?"

I shake my head no. No, Mom, that's not it.

She doesn't get it.

She just doesn't get it.

"Baby, what is it? Should I get the board?"

I nod.

The board.

"The board" is a piece of paper with letters on it. A–Z. This is how we talk to each other. She points to letters, and when she's on the right one, I click my tongue. She writes the letter down. Then begins with the board again.

She's a bad speller so it takes forever.

But it works. It's my only option.

Mom grabs the paper, holds it up, points toward it. "John, take your time. Just tell me what's wrong."

She points to the first row of letters.

A B C D E F G H I

J K L M N O P Q R

S T U V W X Y Z

No.

Then she points at the second row.

Yes.

So I click my tongue.

So she makes her way along the letters. J . . . K . . . L . . . M . . . Click!

M

Then again, she points at the first row, then the second, then the third . . . Click!

She points along the bottom row of letters. S . . . T . . . U . . . V . . . W . . . X . . . Y . . . Click!

MY

It takes forever, but she finally gets the first two words: MY FACE.

Thankfully Mom figures out what I'm worried about before I have to spell any more. "Oh, no, John, it is a miracle, but your face is fine. Please, don't worry. You look just like you always did, just with a lot more bandages around your face."

I don't believe her.

I've heard them say I was burned on my entire body. One hundred percent of it. I know my face is, too.

I squeeze my eyes shut.

I hear some shuffling and hushed voices.

Finally, I sense my mom by my side.

I open my eyes and look over at her.

She's found a mirror.

She wants me to look at my reflection.

I shut my eyes again. I keep them closed. I've seen enough to already know what it will look like.

"John, it's okay, sweet boy. Open your eyes. Your little face is fine. It's perfect."

So I nervously open them.

The mirror is small, round, and rimmed in white plastic; the reflection shows the bandages covering almost everything as they form a frame around my face. A green feeding tube snakes up and into my nose, which is peeling, but my nose is there. My lips are cracked and dry, but they are there, too. What I can see of my cheeks are rosy and flaking. My eyebrows and eyelids are a little singed, but they're there, too.

I can't see much, but what I can see is enough. Mom is right—my face is fine. At least part of me, perhaps the best part of me, is okay.

I am still there. It's still me.

I look away from the mirror and at my parents. Dad is standing right next to Mom. I nod and try to thank them with a click of my tongue.

Then they see something they haven't seen on my face in a while: a smile.

———————

There was a time when my parents weren't sure they'd ever see me smile again.

The morning of the fire, the few minutes we had together in the emergency room was all we had, but it solidified our commitment to fight. Mom and Dad were then ushered out of the room and into a waiting area.

While the staff worked to set up a permanent room, stabilize me, and prepare my body for the journey ahead, my parents anxiously waited. The doctors explained what we faced. They explained the perils awaiting a patient burned on 100 percent of the body. They discussed the transformation of my body, the loss of skin, the bandages to protect against exposure, the intense swelling, and the improbability of my surviving.

Still, nothing prepared Mom and Dad fully for what they saw once they were able to visit me later that afternoon.

In the emergency room they had seen their little boy alert, curious, talkative, hopeful. My eyes were wide-open, my voice raspy, but clear. A light sheet covered my body.

A few hours later everything had changed.

Everything.

My entire body was wrapped in bandages; only a small section of my face was visible. Various machines were monitoring my life signs and beeping warnings. Staff moved busily through the room, desperately trying to keep me alive. They pumped liquids through an IV in hopes of providing much-needed hydration for my parched skin and tissues. As a result of the liquids, my body was bloated. My head was melon shaped. My eyes were swollen shut. My arms and legs were strapped down to the bed forming an X preventing any kind of movement. Because of damage to my lungs, I was intubated. A hole had been cut in my throat to force oxygen into my smoke-damaged lungs and made talking impossible.

This is what my parents walked into.

This was their child lying asleep—sedated, mummified, and strapped down.

This was our new life.

Hearing the warnings and prognosis and odds was one thing. But to see me like this was overwhelming. They had a few minutes to whisper encouragement, pat my bandaged head, and tell me they loved me. As quickly as they were escorted in, Mom and Dad were ushered away so that the staff could ready me for my first surgery.

The gravitas of the situation overwhelmed my parents.

Mom went to the chapel to pray.

Dad went outside to cry.

The journey forward seemed impossibly grim.

Yet those bandages that encapsulated me that first afternoon effectively did their job for the next five months.

Those wrappings helped keep my body free from infection. They allowed the slow regrowth of my skin. They provided safe harbor during those months in the hospital and the opportunity for dozens of surgeries. They protected me from the great risk of death as life slowly returned.

Even after I left the hospital, those bandages remained to cover the areas of my body still damaged, still open, still wounded.

Eight months after being wrapped in those grave garments I was finally set free.

The final wounds had healed.

The last wrapping was removed.

There was no need for Silvadene.

There was no need for bandages.

There was no need to stay covered up.

It was now healthy to let my skin feel the air. It was now time to let those scars see the light.

Although the bandages were removed, I remained covered up.

I traded in the bandages intended to protect open sores for bandages that covered up a painful past, difficult present, and uncertain future. You see, in that moment when Mom brought that mirror to me, when I saw my face was okay? It was an inflection point. I decided that when I got out of the hospital, instead of sharing the miracle of my recovery, which would have meant exposing my wounds, I was going to pretend that everything else was okay, too. I was going to pretend that I had never been burned.

To fit in I wore long sleeves and pants year-round so that no one could see my scars. I wanted to have normal skin, normal hands, a normal life, like other kids. I didn't like my wheelchair; I didn't like ankles that barely bent and joints that were locked in place. I hated that my arms and legs had lost all their fat, all their muscle, leaving me bone skinny.

So I covered up.

I remained bound with self-imposed bandages. Not just for that first summer. But for the two decades that followed.

MASKING UP

Plucking hairs. Smearing foundation. Waxing eyebrows. Curling eyelashes. Whitening teeth.

We spend hours each week staring into a mirror preparing ourselves for the day, getting ready for the meeting, prepping for the date.

There is absolutely nothing wrong with a little enhancement of our natural beauty. But all too often we aren't trying to enhance what we see in the reflection; we are carefully constructing a mask to cover up what we don't think will be embraced by the world at large.

Like circus performers, we smear on makeup to become someone else. Far beyond applying a little lip gloss or hair dye, our mask attempts to cover up who we really are. Our mask covers what we've been through, what we know to be important, and what we are afraid to share with others. Our mask hides our scars, our unique stories, our regrets, and our dreams. It covers up our shame and our brokenness.

It stifles our potential.

It covers up the best of who we are.

It masks the glow that we can offer others.

It hides the light we can reflect to a world starved for it.

It censors the story that uniquely sets us apart and would, if shared, intimately connect us with others.

My mask affected my behavior after getting out of the hospital, in grade school, in middle school, and beyond.

Mom and Dad, please don't read the next few paragraphs.

Okay.

Now that they're not reading, I can let you know that in high school and college, I was not particularly gifted in arts, music, class work, or sports. I didn't have a job, didn't date, wasn't on fire in my faith or secure with who I was. I desperately needed something to get noticed.

So I picked out and put on a new mask.

The mask covered my scars, connected me with others, and freed me to excel at something: drinking.

I lived for the weekends.

And in college the word *weekend* meant Wednesday through Sunday.

Not dating, not working, and not trying too hard in class, not being grounded in something greater than myself, I strived to go out more frequently, drink faster, consume more, and stay out later than any of my friends.

Not only did I try. I succeeded.

It was immature. It was dangerous. It was stupid.

And it was a coping mechanism.

For me, the buzz, the real addiction, wasn't as much about the alcohol as it was the sense of being accepted, of belonging, of being seen.

Of being just like everyone else.

Of being loved.

GET OVER IT

When I was growing up, so desperate to be seen as a normal kid, I believed my value came from the perspective of others.

Crazy, I know.

Here's the thing, though: to various degrees, I think we all believe this. When we're growing up, we are easily influenced by our friends and what they think of us.

Who remembers all those assemblies in junior high about peer pressure? I know I do. I'm sure I was sitting with my friends, throwing spitballs, ignoring the presenter, and trying to be cool. Essentially, doing exactly what they were encouraging us not to do.

We know peer pressure is real. We're comfortable admitting we succumbed to it in school. We remember trying to figure out who we were and what group we best fit into. We tried all different kinds of masks back then . . . athlete, Goth, band kid, drama club. We laugh about it now.

But what we don't realize is that this is one phase . . . we never outgrew.

Think about it.

We're still trying to figure out who we are and what group we best fit into. We still long to sit at the right tables, get a ton of "likes," hang with the right groups, be invited to the right parties, make the right amount of money, and be seen with the right people.

We graduated high school.

But we haven't gotten over it.

An entire industry is even devoted to keeping that pressure on us.

All advertisements make us wonder . . . are we keeping up? Are we fitting in? What do we need to make sure we're *really* accepted?

Sure, the advertising industry exists to sell stuff. But their job, their reason for being, is to sow the seeds of discontent in each of us—and promote their product as the solution to what ails us.

Why do you think so many people rack up credit-card debt? That's one of the costs of all those masks.

So we buy in. And we mask up.

We do what we want others to see.

We're not afraid of who we are. We're afraid of who we think we're not.

We strive, then, not to become the best version of ourselves. We strive instead for what we think will make us most worthy in the eyes and opinions of others.

But in the end, we're still too fat, still too old, still too poor, still too wrinkly, still too unconnected, still too broken. The comparison we make to magazine covers, idealistic lives, and "perfect" neighbors is one we lose.

Always.

I now believe that we were made perfectly in the image of God. Perfectly. Dimples, pimples, scars and all. The only comparison that matters is the comparison with who you are, who you were, and who you could become.

I was so afraid to see my reflection in that room thirty years ago. I was so afraid that I would always be seen as different. *Oh, there goes that kid that got burned.* I could hear the taunts in my head already.

But by denying what happened to me, I denied the world the chance to hear about the miracle of my survival, the wonder of my life, and the magnificent potential of theirs.

THE RED JACKET

I trained to be a hospital chaplain when I was twenty-seven.

I hadn't planned on doing it. But I stumbled into it, and once I start something, I usually don't stop.

Despite a successful career as a real estate developer, I had always dreamed of somehow working on a college campus. I loved my time at Saint Louis University and had on occasion considered going back to work with students.

One night while surfing their website I saw a link about the SLU chaplaincy training program. I thought, *Perfect! Work with students, help them figure out why they are here, what to major in, how to move through adversity, and encourage them to pursue what matters in life. Awesome!* I filled out the application that evening, hit SUBMIT, and didn't think much else about it. Two weeks later I received a call that I'd been accepted into the program.

Amazing.

This was going to rock.

Time to change lives, baby!

But I hadn't read the fine print.

The program's focus was on becoming a hospital chaplain. Completion of the program wouldn't let me encourage and inspire students, but would teach me how to go in and comfort and console people in their scariest and darkest moments in the hospital.

Oops.

Our individual strengths and weaknesses are typically just different sides of the same coin. I'm not a quitter. Which means even though I knew this program wasn't for me, even though it was leading me down a path I'd never even considered, even though it was a huge time commitment for a year, I refused to drop out.

I went through the classes.

Worked the overnight shifts.

Completed the intense workload.

And the experiences during the program, and the three years I spent serving as a part-time chaplain afterward, blessed and transformed my life. Far from a mistake, it was a time of incredible growth and discovery.

Frequently our apparent mistakes give birth to our biggest blessings.

After each visit with a patient in the hospital, we would meet with an adviser to debrief our effectiveness. These meetings would help improve our focus, communication, and impact. Being invited to sit, speak, and listen to grieving, ill, anxious, lonely, or dying patients was a massive honor; it was totally humbling. But those visits were frequently challenging and exhausting to me as well.

After one particularly difficult session with a patient, I was talking about what happened with my adviser, Dr. Davis. He sat patiently and listened. He leaned back in his chair. He put his hands behind his head. He asked a few clarifying questions.

Then he said, "John, do you know what your story is?"

I looked at him briefly, puzzled.

This wasn't about me. This was about the person I was trying to help!

Plus, hadn't he listened to anything I'd said these past few months? He knew I'd grown up in the area and had attended SLU as an undergrad.

He looked at me. "Seriously, John, tell me your story."

Um, well, I grew up here in St. Louis. I work as a real estate developer—

He interrupted me. "No, John. Do you know what *your* story is?"

I paused, still confused as to what he was after.

Okay, I'll go further back. I'm one of six kids, my parents met in high school and are still married—

This time he interrupted me by getting up from his chair, walking over to a cabinet, and paging through the files.

I stopped talking and crossed my arms in frustration.

Finally he found what he was looking for, pulled out a sheet of paper, and handed it to me. "Read this."

I took the sheet of paper and begrudgingly began to read.

Though it's been over ten years since I read it, I will never forget the story.

The article was about a little girl who walked into a classroom, took off the bright red jacket she had been wearing, threw it on the floor, then sat down at her desk. The teacher saw what she did and asked the girl, Mary, if she could please go hang her jacket up.

The little girl looked at the jacket, back at the teacher, and said, "That's not my jacket."

The teacher explained that it wasn't a big deal, Mary wasn't in trouble, but that she saw the little girl drop the jacket and she needed to go hang it up in the back of the room.

The little girl argued back, "That's not my jacket. I told you, it's not mine."

A classmate piped in, "But I saw you drop it. It's the jacket you wear every single day, Mary."

The little girl crossed her arms, stomped her feet, and yelled back, "That's not my jacket. That's not my jacket!"

I finished the article, handed it back, and looked up blankly at Dr. Davis.

"Do you understand what that story is saying?"

Um, that this little girl needs to hang up her freaking jacket?

Dr. Davis shook his head. "John, we all have a story. We all have unique experiences that make us who we are. Those experiences create the gift that you, specifically, and only you, can share with others." He paused. "John, I don't know why you decided to start this program, or what your gift is, but just know that you can't possibly help those people lying in the hospital beds identify what matters most to them if you don't first know your story, what you've been through and what matters most to you."

Although I graduated from the chaplaincy program, I still had no clue what that red-jacket story or that little girl had to do with me.

I am a slow learner.

Fortunately, the people who knew me best were about to rock my world by putting my red jacket in a place where I could no longer cross my arms in denial. Whether I liked it or not, my red jacket was about to be forced on, zipped up, glued on, and broadcast loudly to the whole classroom and the entire world.

MASK OFF; RED JACKET ON

As a family, mine never discussed the fire.

We endured it, survived it, and moved past it. We chose not to be defined by it.

That is, until my parents sat in the first row of a church on November 22, 2003.

Their older son, Jim, stood on the altar in a tuxedo, the best man for their younger, better-looking son, John.

Watching their boys together, with their four daughters as bridesmaids, and a gorgeous woman in white named Beth about to join the family, they realized something for the first time: the terrible fire from years earlier wasn't the end. The tragedy we'd endured as a family decades ago had a happy ending.

The fire did not take away the life their little boy could make for himself. Contrarily, it led perfectly to this place, this church, this altar, this union, this day.

The therapy and surgeries and amputations and scars and challenges culminated in a blowout celebration. It was miracle upon miracle upon miracle.

If you ever meet my wife, you, too, will know it's a miracle.

The little burned boy was blessed. My wife is a knockout. Inside and out.

At the end of the service, as Beth and I walked together down the aisle, my parents were overflowing with gratitude to my doctors, to their family and friends who supported them, and most of all to God, whom we credit with the miracle of not only my survival, but an incredible life just beginning. It is our belief that God works through all things for a perfect purpose, that everything in the end is made new, and that even a terrible childhood fire is used for good.

Within a week they were writing a book about their experience years earlier.

It was *their* story as parents experiencing the devastating news that *their* son had been burned. It was *their* story about months of waiting-room anguish, support from the community, and a miraculous triumph.

Yeah, it was *their* story . . . but they planned to put a picture of me on the cover.

The picture was one taken of me shortly after leaving the hospital. It shows a young boy with a baseball cap on and bright red scarring on his face and neck. It shows a kid with a thick white brace on his neck, a dip in his throat from a recent tracheotomy and splints on his arms.

That photo had always reminded me of all that made me different. It reinforced how the fire had disfigured me and how I had spent the twenty years after it striving to be ordinary. It reminded me of my years longing to look and act and be like everybody else. It reminded me of my failure to fit in and my inability to blend in with everyone else.

I hated that picture.

In the early stages of their book writing, I was far from encouraging. I didn't believe there was a story to tell and encouraged them not to dredge up the past. I offered my best arguments against it. Who will read your book? Why would they care? Do you guys even know how to use a computer? I suggested they keep the story in their hearts.

They wrote their book.

They called it *Overwhelming Odds*.

They ignored my advice.

Jerks.

And in doing so, they changed my life.

Imagine this: the mask you've so carefully constructed to hide behind your entire life is removed. You know, the one that tells the world you're fine, you're all good, your kids are perfect, you have no problems, there are no addictions, no worries, no scars? Imagine that it is taken gently off your face, set carefully on a table, and smashed with a massive sledgehammer.

Now the entire world could see and read all about the real me, the broken me.

I felt exposed.

But as I continued to read, I realized something else.

For the first time I understood that I wasn't the only one burned in the story. For the first time I came to understand all that my family went through. My brother, Jim, was injured physically and emotionally. My sisters were prescribed sleeping pills because of witnessing me burning in front of them and the months of constant fear that they'd lose me for good. Oh, and my parents. My poor parents. As difficult as my physical pain was, the emotional toll on them was, in so many ways, much worse.

Imagine also learning that your story somehow galvanized a community into action. Our neighbors opened up their homes to my siblings as we waited for the house to be repaired; the community raised money, donated blood, offered prayers, brought food. I had never before fully considered all the people who came together to make the miracle a reality.

And imagine, after reading the last page of your tragic story, seeing it differently, clearly for the first time. As if cataracts had been cut away, I understood, *Oh my gosh . . . it was all a gift.*

The fire.

The hospitalization.

The pain.

The fears.

The amputations.

The scars.

All of it was a gift.

All of it.

The fire led perfectly to where I am today. The challenges led to experiences that shaped me, the character that drives me, the faith that guides me, the life around me, and to the possibility in front of me.

No, it wasn't always perfect.

It wasn't always the life I wanted.

But it was my life.

It was my story.

It was my red jacket.

And it was time to claim it.

Now, this is important: the red jacket is worn not to seek sympathy, but to free you from longing for it. You may want to read that again.

It's not worn to perpetually remind others about your brutal childhood, lousy marriage, crummy health, shabby job, or rotten life. It's certainly not worn as a crutch as to why you remain stuck in the rut today. Nope, we wear it proudly to learn the lessons within it, celebrate the scars resulting from it, and do even greater things because of it.

And so we choose to embrace our story. We acknowledge the brutal scars. After reading my parents' book, the scars that I had been covering up for twenty years were transformed into badges of honor.

The scars remained, yes. But they were there because the wounds had healed.

They were evidence of a miracle.

Covering them up denied others the chance to see them.

To question.

To connect.

To share.

To grow.

To live.

To shine.

After I read my parents' book, I turned the book over and stared at the picture on the cover.

The picture of me as a kid with my scars and splints was still there. But now, I saw something I had never seen before: unbridled hope. I saw a little boy who was a bit beaten down physically, but who was choosing not to be defined by it. I saw an enormous smile and eyes that exuded joy. I no longer saw a little boy at the end of a journey he had barely survived, but instead at the start of one that he could not wait to begin.

DISCOVERING GOLD

Have you ever heard of the Phra Phuttha Maha Suwan Patimakon?

Me either.

That is, until recently. While at a speaking engagement in Bangkok, Thailand, a driver shared with me what it was, why it matters, and why it was one place I had to go.

Apparently, seven hundred years ago a massive golden statue was molded into the image of Buddha. Almost ten feet tall and weighing eleven thousand pounds, it was the largest golden statue in the world. Dwelling in a modest temple, it inspired and was revered for hundreds of years.

In the mid-1700s though, with Burmese invaders approaching, the monks of the temple devised a plan to save their cherished golden Buddha. Knowing that if the invaders discovered it, they would steal it, the monks quickly covered the entire statue with thick plaster. Shards of colored glass were inlaid. The spectacular sculpture was quickly transformed into something ordinary.

Its true value was successfully hidden from the invaders, who never guessed what was beneath the plaster.

The inner beauty was kept from those invaders.

And then from the world.

For two hundred years!

In 1954, a mighty, ancient, plastered, but underwhelming statue was to be moved to a new location. The statue had been in the temple for as long as records had been kept.

While a team was slowly lifting the form off the ground, their ropes broke from its weight. The statue fell to the ground. A small crack formed.

The team saw a glimmering reflection from within the crack.

They chipped away a little.

And then a little more. Slowly, the stunning majesty of the golden Buddha, whose full splendor had been masked for two centuries, was revealed.

What was once kept under a leaky tin roof in a seldom-visited temple has been transported to one of the most celebrated and visited locations in all of Bangkok. Brilliance that was once masked is now again on display for the world to see.

This amazing story speaks to a truth that is within each of

our stories. Not only does each have incredible worth and beauty, but the world is desperate to be inspired by it.

It's time to chip away the plaster, pull down the mask, peel off the bandages, and allow the miracle of your life to shine brightly.

If you want to live a radically inspired life, it's time to embrace your story and to celebrate the amazing miracle of your life.

I don't know your specific story, but I do know we've all been burned, dealt with struggle, and endured storms. We've lost parents, children, and friends. We've failed in businesses, marriages, and dreams. We've stumbled spiritually, physically, and financially.

Yet our scars from these experiences, when we learn from them, aren't signs of weakness to be covered up, but symbols of strength to be celebrated.

They are darkened and useless when covered.

They are illuminative and inspiring when exposed.

DROP THE ACT

I typically start my workshops for business leaders with brief introductions.

People tend to share their name, their company, what they do, how many employees they have. All superficial stuff. No real depth. No authentic connection. No personal truth.

So I always do a second round of introductions.

I don't let things stay at that first level. I want people to take off the masks. I do something simple that immediately allows the conversations to go deeper, the tone in the room to change, and relationships to begin to grow.

"Okay, okay, nice to meet you all. Now that I know less about you after you shared than before, let's do this again. I want you to go around the room again and share something else. What if we were actually friends? What if we were really doing life together? What if the conversation actually mattered, this day actually meant something? Now finish this sentence: *John, if you really knew me, you'd know that . . .*"

Knowing that everybody has a story, and it's usually not the one they are sharing with the world, I want them to go deeper, to feel more, to share more, to live more.

I'll never forget the first time I did this exercise and asked this question with a group of twelve business owners in Miami, Florida. I asked the gentleman to my left to begin and we went around the room afterward. He stood, looked at me, and shared, *Beneath the nice suit and confident manner, I have no clue what to do next in my business . . . and even less of an idea what to do with my fifteen-year-old son.*

He sat down.

The room changed. You could feel it. Arms were being uncrossed. Hearts were beginning to open. The room was charged with possibility. The light was beginning to shine.

The next person stood up. *I am hypersensitive to the way my kids, friends, and employees treat one another because of the way I was treated as a child.*

Now we were rolling. The conversation had shifted from

being superficial to being authentic and life-giving. We went one by one through the room with each leader sharing:

A woman shared: *I have a void in my life because of my inability to have children.*

Another offered: *I am a mother today of a five-year-old because four years ago my brother and his wife died in a car accident.*

A young man said: *I am funny but no one knows it because I am shy.*

And then we came to the final gentleman. He stood, made eye contact with every person sitting in the room, and then shared slowly:

When I was seven, my father was murdered. And my mother and I were both . . . grateful.

Even I was shocked at this man's willingness to admit not only to us, but to himself, how he and his mom had felt back then.

This one man lowered his mask. He shared his life honestly. I'm not sure he'd ever told anyone that before. But that glimmer of truth lit up the whole room.

Henri Nouwen, one of my favorite writers, says, "We like to make a distinction between our private and public lives and say 'whatever I do in my private life is nobody else's business.' But anyone trying to live a spiritual life will soon discover that the most personal is the most universal, the most hidden is the most public. . . ."

The most solitary is the most communal.

The most inner light is a light for the world.

Those times where we were broken and healed are the spaces that connect us to our fellow humans. We may have grown up in different neighborhoods and gone to different schools. We have different jobs and different families. But we all know the pain of loneliness; we all know the fear of being unloved.

Those are the places that can bring us together. So often we push people away, afraid that they don't want to see the hard stuff. But the hard stuff is what we should be doing together. It is what joins us as humans.

This is an inflection point for you whether you know it or not. Every moment is. This is your chance to realize that when you are going through the hard stuff, you are not alone.

Have you had a hard day at the office and feel beat down and as if you want to quit? You can keep your mask held high and suffer alone. Or you can put the mask down and talk to your spouse about how you are really feeling.

Are your kids driving you crazy? You find yourself pulling out your hair and it's barely lunchtime? You can let it out on your kids, feeling frustrated and lonely, or you can call your neighbor down the street. Share your struggles and your heart and find true connection.

Are you feeling that too much is going on, that you are stressed to the max and you just can't handle it? You can just keep plowing forward, completely spent, burned-out, yet hiding how much you hurt. Or you can text a friend, share your burden, and realize that he or she feels the same way.

That's where real life is lived. Over coffee in the front yard, and over the pillow at the end of the day. In the moments when we let our guard down and open our lives and hearts. Let our light shine so it can illuminate the darkness others are feeling.

And I've discovered that in lowering my mask and letting others into the deepest corners of my heart, that far from pushing me away, they'll frequently respond with the beautiful words, "You too?"

But that can't happen if you are pretending your life is Instagram perfect, creating a facade that prevents others from ever seeing the real you.

Living life on fire means you aren't afraid to know and *own* your story; you celebrate the scars you've accumulated along the way, and you are ready and willing to live life honestly.

Otherwise you'll never know the gift of your story.

You won't know the power of your experiences.

You can't embrace the beauty of your scars.

You'll never be a light to a world desperate for it.

LOVING IT

Sometimes we need another set of eyes to remind us how beautiful those scars really are.

One morning, I was getting ready for work, shaving in the bathroom as my son Jack watched, standing perched on the toilet seat. I'd given him a razor with a plastic shield on it and watched as he modeled my motions. When I shaved my left side, he shaved his left. When I switched to my right, Jack switched, too. Then he stopped moving his hands. He stopped shaving, and I noticed he was staring at my torso. Now, understand that my entire body is terribly scarred, but on no place on my body are the scars thicker, more obvious than on my stomach.

As I continued shaving, I could see his little mind working. He came down from the toilet, walked over, and looked up at me. He raised his hand, tracked one of my scars with his index finger, and said, "Daddy?"

Yeah, buddy, what is it?

I braced for the awkward question or conversation we were about to have . . . started thinking of ways to answer his question . . . how much detail about the fire . . . how much information about the burns . . . how should he share with his friends what had happened to his dad . . . how to tell him he didn't need to be embarrassed or scared . . .

"Daddy, your tummy is red, it's bumpy, and it's ridgey . . ."

Then added, "and I *love* it!"

You know, Jack, I love it, too.

DENIAL V. SELF-ACCEPTANCE

Where there is ruin, there is hope for treasure.
—Rumi

What's your story?

Not the one you share at cocktail parties. Not what's printed on your résumé or the one you feature on your online profile.

It's time to drop the act and take off the mask.

It's time to dare to believe that who you are underneath is enough.

Because it is.

My challenge to you is, as you look in the mirror, at your reflection, at your day, at your life, to confidently recognize that you and your story are priceless.

This time don't cover up, but marvel.

No one else has your story, your scars, your wisdom.

No one.

Embrace them.

Accept them.

Learn from them and celebrate them.

You wouldn't be here without them.

Your reflection may be a bit red, bumpy, and ridgey, but it's led you perfectly to where you are today—and the possibility of what you can do next. So rip off the bandages. Take off the mask. Look in the mirror. Love what you see. Smile at the reflection. And share it with others.

Choose self-acceptance.

Faith is remembering in the darkness

what we have experienced in the light.

—RICHARD ROHR

3

ARE YOU ALL IN?

*Extinguish indifference, ignite potential, and discover
the power of a purposeful life.*

*I*t will get better.

Mom and Dad keep saying this to me.

*They keep telling me that we'll be able to take the trach out of my
throat soon—and then I'll be able to talk again.*

*They keep telling me that pretty soon I'll be well enough so they
can allow more visitors in—and then I won't be so bored.*

*They keep telling me that I'm getting better—and then I'll be able
to go home.*

*But some days it's just hard being tied down to this bed, unable to
do a thing, stuck in so much pain.*

Some days it doesn't feel as if it's ever going to get better.

This is one of those days.

Trying to encourage me, Mom starts reading one of the cards that came in the mail.

This is always a good part of the day. We get a whole box of cards every day now. People all over the world are writing. It's pretty cool.

We get letters from kids in schools and old people from churches. We don't know how everyone knows about what happened to me, but people everywhere seem to be thinking about and praying for us. We even got a letter from the White House signed by President Reagan. And we got one from the Vatican.

They don't make the day easier, but how many other kids have their room wallpapered in get-well cards? How many other kids got a letter from the pope?!

With Mom opening the mail and reading to me, Dad gets up.

He comes over and kisses my head.

He says he'll be right back and leaves the room.

Mom stays.

She keeps reading the cards aloud.

A few minutes later the big glass door to my room slides open.

Dad is back.

"John, there is a special visitor that really wanted to see you today."

I see a guy walk in wearing a yellow hospital gown, yellow bootees, yellow mask, yellow hat, and rubber gloves.

Mom and Dad always wear this outfit. The doctors and the nurses always wear this outfit, too. They all wear it so I don't get an infection.

I'm used to them coming in and out of my room.

But this person is new. I can just tell.

Nothing fits right on him.

Everything is masked except his eyes. He kinda looks like a big, yellow burglar.

He's walking closer.

I don't know who it is.

Until I hear his voice.

"How you doing, little Chester?"

Oh my gosh.

Only one person would call me that stupid name.

My brother, Jim, gave me this nickname when I was little.

I hated it.

I told him to stop.

He never did.

And I hated him every time he said it.

I'd fight him anytime he called me it.

So my jerk brother would just call me it even more.

But this time, when I hear that name, I'm not mad.

I don't want to fight him.

I don't want to punch him.

I don't hate him.

I want to get out of this bed and hug him. I want to use my voice and thank him.

The last time I saw Jim was the day of the fire.

He tried to get in the back of the ambulance to ride with me to the hospital, but the ambulance guy didn't let him.

The man shut the left door.

I begged the guy to let Jim in. I told him that he was my brother and I needed him to come, too. I couldn't go by myself.

The guy said he was sorry. Then he shut the other door. He yelled, Let's go. And we pulled away.

Man, I had never felt so alone. Looking out a little, rectangular window in the ambulance, a stranger asking me questions, watching Jim standing on the street, hands on his hips, watching us leave, I was so scared.

Ever since that moment I've wanted to tell Jim something. For several weeks now I've wanted to tell him.

I click Dad to get my alphabet board.

He grabs it. Points to the first row of letters, then the second, then the third.

A B C D E F G H I

J K L M N O P Q R

S T U V W X Y Z

I click. So he makes his way along the third. S . . . T . . . U . . . V . . . W . . . X . . . Y . . . CLICK!

Y

He writes the letter down.

Then again, he starts pointing at the first row, then the second. CLICK!

J . . . K . . . L . . . M . . . N . . . O . . . CLICK!

YO

Again he points at the first row, then the second, and the third. CLICK!

S . . . T . . . U . . . CLICK!

Got the first word out: YOU.

I look away from the letter board and up at my brother. Although everything else is masked and covered, I can see Jim's eyes.

And his eyes are smiling.

I look back at the board, and with Dad's help I click out the second word: SAVED.

I had never known if Jim liked me.

He was eight years older than I was. He could be such a jerk sometimes. Not letting me hang out with his friends, calling me mean names, making me smell his socks after he mowed the lawn.

But lying there in bed, looking up at Jim, thinking about all he'd done for me, I realized something else about him:

He liked me.

No, he actually loved me.

And there was no doubt that he was now my hero.

I finish the last word: ME.

YOU SAVED ME.

Jim shook his head. "Oh, I didn't save you. You are the real hero. You're doing the real hard work. Now get better soon, little Chester."

NO. YOU SAVED ME.

What comes to mind when you hear the word *hero*?

Maybe you think of superheroes.

Superman?

Batman?

Wonder Woman?

Maybe you think of someone in the news like Captain Chesley Sullenberger, who safely landed his aircraft on the Hudson River, saving the lives of all the people on the flight.

Who else comes to mind?

Firefighters, police officers, our armed forces?

Yes, heroes can certainly be people who put their own lives at risk to save others. Those who step in, act bravely, lead selflessly, even when confronted with fear. They can be the ones racing forward when everyone else is running away.

But most heroes aren't always super. Most don't live in comic books or headlines.

Most are very human, go unheralded, and look much more like Clark Kent than Superman.

They're ordinary; a lot like you and me.

And what an incredible example I saw in action the day I was burned.

SEMPER FIDELIS

Always Faithful.

This is the motto of the US Marine Corps.

I'm blessed to speak at the FOCUS Marines Foundation events every quarter, and then to personally visit with these heroes for several hours afterward. It's the professional highlight of my year. Over the past five years of partnering with them I've discovered that, for marines, *Semper Fi* isn't just a catchy phrase, but a way of life.

The foundation started with a few retired marines who saw a need to support soldiers returning from war. The group understood that for many veterans the battles don't end when they return home.

Traumatic brain injury.

Post-traumatic stress disorder.

Survivor's guilt.

Physical injuries.

Unemployment.

Addictions.

Hopelessness.

These are some of the challenges facing several hundred thousand veterans. Each quarter, a few dozen brave warriors, tired of barely living leave their homes, travel to Missouri, and gather in a remote location. Pulled away from the busyness of their lives, placed into the beauty of nature, these heroes learn crucial skills in coping with grief, harnessing emotion, and growing professionally. They also realize their deployment may have ended, but their most important fight remains.

At the most recent gathering, I asked a gentleman from Alabama what had been the best part of the week. He said that it felt good to be alive again.

What does that mean, to be alive again?

He responded, "I used to know when I was going to wake up and where I'd eat breakfast. I knew each day would be busy, that the danger was real, but that I had guys there to watch my back, I was there to watch their backs. I knew what work had to be done and that the work we did mattered.

"But when I returned to my 'real' life, my life after serving, all of that was gone. I didn't care anymore about anyone or anything. I didn't know what I was fighting for. I almost lost my life. But this week, I got it back. I'm alive again. I'm alive again. And it feels f#¢!ing awesome."

As active marines, these incredible men and women were driven forward by a strong sense of mission. They knew the value of being Always Faithful. They lived it every day.

Once back home, though, some struggle without the tight fellowship and compelling purpose. Without a mission they can become completely unmoored.

There's nothing like a new mission to remind us of what's worth fighting for.

I've experienced it transform the lives of these brave marines.

And I experienced it radically change my brother's life, too.

As a seventeen-year-old boy, Jim was a typical teenager, focused on himself. He was likely concerned about what kind of car he'd like to own someday, or what girl he'd like to take to the prom, or scoring the occasional six-pack to split among seven friends.

Teenagers have a reputation for being selfish, rebellious, having attitude. They pretend to be too cool to care. They step back. They retreat into their rooms, their headphones, their technology, their own lives.

Some of it is understandable. They are learning to be independent in the world. They are pushing their family unit away, anticipating the future when they won't have that family to fall back on. But it spawns an attitude of indifference, a life outlook that shrugs, saying, *So what? I don't care, whatever. So what that my room is a mess, so what that you are yelling at me. So what, who cares, I'm above all this.*

But Jim stopped shrugging the morning I was burned.

He had a mission. His little brother was on fire. He had a choice. *Save your brother. Or watch him die.*

What he did next would change his life.

And mine.

I remember the day I was burned with absolute vividness.

I remember the explosion. The detonation that split the gas can in two, blasted me against the far side of the garage, blew out windows in the garage and rattled neighbors' houses blocks away.

I remember my ears ringing, smoke alarms screaming, and the odd, muffled growl of fire crackling like when one is burning in a fireplace. The sound, that snapping and hissing, was all around me; it was all over me.

I remember running through the flames in the garage to a doorway leading back to the house. Once inside and still on fire, I ran through the kitchen, family room, and into the front hall.

I stood in the hallway on fire.

In pain.

Terrified.

Screaming and praying for someone, anyone, to come and save me.

And I remember seeing Jim running toward me.

This is the guy who gives me nicknames I hate. This is the guy who makes me peanut-butter-and-jelly sandwiches . . . laced with Tabasco sauce. This is the guy who hates when I am around him. This is a typical older brother.

So standing in the front hall burning and pleading and praying for a hero, it wasn't exactly Jim I imagined coming to my rescue. No, I imagined a firefighter, my dad, a neighbor, a hero, someone, anyone, who could really help me. Not Jim!

Ah, but this was his inflection point. This was his moment. This was his chance to change, to step forward, to move swiftly, to act courageously, and to risk his life for mine.

Jim ran around me, shielding his face with one hand to protect himself from the flames leaping from my body. He picked up the front-hall floor mat, advanced toward me, and began beating my body with it.

Each time he swung down, the flames leaped from me toward him.

It became too painful, too hard, too much.

After several swings of the mat into my body, he pulled back.

He stopped swinging.

He dropped the mat.

STEPPING INTO THE FIRE

Jim had a choice that morning.

Pull back when the fire got too hot, let me burn, and save himself.

Or step back into the fight, get burned, and try to save me.

He did what I think most would do. He pulled back.

Think about it. Have you ever touched anything hot? When you do, what's your natural response?

You pull back.

What do you say?

Ouch.

Now, c'mon, what do you really say?

Okay, you know what, I don't care what you say.

Words are cheap; actions are what matter. In life, it matters much less what we say than what we do.

When things get hot, when the fires of life rage around you and against you, you can pull back and retreat and let things be destroyed.

Or, you can step back in and save what matters from the fires that are threatening to destroy your marriage, your career, your joy, your life.

The key to that choice, the only way to reengage in the fight, is in knowing, without a doubt, why you are doing it.

One of my favorite quotes about that comes from Patanjali. He wrote in the second century BC:

When you are inspired by some great purpose, some
    extraordinary project,
all your thoughts break their bonds.
Your mind transcends limitations,
your consciousness expands in every direction,
and you find yourself in a new, great, and wonderful world.
Dormant forces, faculties, and talents become alive,
and you discover yourself to be a greater person by far
than you ever dreamed yourself to be.

It's a marvelous quote. Each word beautiful, every sentence poetic, and all of it true.

It's important to realize, though, that as wonderful as it is, the entirety of it hinges on the first line: "When you are inspired by some great purpose . . ."

We all want the rest of the quote, we want the good stuff. We certainly want our thoughts to break their bonds so that we can enthusiastically imagine, collaborate, initiate, and create. We long to live in a new, great, and wonderful world.

But we don't get any of it until we are "inspired by some great purpose," until we know what it is that makes us become fully alive. Until we have that thing, that cause, that person, worth fighting for, we'll just be stuck saying, *So what?*

That thing, that cause, that person.

To live a radically inspired life, you must choose to go All In each day with a purpose greater than yourself.

After having put down the rug, Jim watched as the flames continued to leap from my body.

He reached back down, picked back up the mat, and stepped back into the fight.

Jim swung down, trying to suffocate the flames dancing on my body.

Then he swung down again.

And again.

He beat the flames down enough to wrap me in the mat and carry me outside. He laid me on the wet, snowy ground and rolled around on top of me. He put out the fire.

With first-degree burns on his hands and arms, Jim then went back into the smoke-filled house, called 911, and checked to make sure everyone else was out of the house.

That morning he became a bigger person by far than he had ever dreamed himself to be.

He saved me.

He became a hero.

NEVER LET GO

Jim wasn't the only one.

As he disappeared back into the burning house to call 911, two of my sisters, Amy, eleven, and Susan, eight, rushed outside. The explosion jarred them from their sleep. When they ran out of their bedroom and down the stairs, they saw me in the hallway, engulfed in flames, screaming. They witnessed Jim savagely beating me with a mat attempting to suffocate those flames. They followed Jim as he carried me outside. And beheld me in the front yard, hunched over, with my clothes and skin dripping off.

Seriously, you just read that and moved on to the next sentence?

Read it again.

Imagine this: Imagine waking up to a thunderous explosion in your house, windows breaking and alarms screaming. Imagine looking down the steps and seeing your brother like a torch burning in front of you. Imagine gasping as you make your way through a smoky house toward the front door. Imagine racing outside, barefoot, in a nightgown, standing in the snow. And imagine seeing your little brother, the one you played with yesterday and fought with last night, a few feet from you burned up, bent over, writhing in pain.

What would you have done?

How would you have responded?

I don't know about you, but I would have taken off running in the opposite direction.

That's me.

I know I would have been too scared to do anything but race from the problem. Or to run to someone else for help. It's the way I handled things as a kid. When I'm honest about it, I realize it's sometimes the way I deal with things today.

Don't we all?

Withdrawing. That's one way to handle the challenges in life. But there is a better way.

The alternative path is to confront, to own, to step in, to serve. Fortunately for me, Amy chose that path.

She immediately came over to me, put her arms around me, pulled me in tight, and said, "It's going to be okay, John. It's going to be okay. Have faith and fight."

Now listen, this was not what I expected from her.

This just isn't what is expected from an eleven-year-old.

I believe those were divinely inspired words and daringly courageous actions that morning. But I wasn't ready for them. I didn't think she was right.

Upon hearing them, I looked down.

And when I did, I saw my hands.

My fingers were constricted into a fist. The skin was red and otherworldly, and I was unable to move my fingers. My arms were flaking and were a blend of bright red hues and charcoal black. My clothes and my skin had become one. I felt my body slowly curling and tightening up even as I stood in her embrace. *It was not going to be okay.*

Then I looked up. There was my childhood home. This beautiful, two-story house held almost every memory from my life. Breakfast gatherings, Thanksgiving dinners, Christmas mornings, birthday celebrations, nightly family dinners, and the going-to-bed arguments that tended to follow. This house was my life. I loved it.

Flames were now leaping from the garage roof; smoke was pouring out of the windows and the front door. I'd ignited these flames; I'd fanned this smoke.

It was more than I could take.

Between the anguish of letting my entire family down and the physical pain of my burns, I looked away from the house. I looked at Amy. I bawled at her, "Amy, I need you to do me a favor. Go back into the house. I don't care if it's on fire. Go into the kitchen, get me a knife, come back out here, and kill me. Amy, just kill me!"

I'll tell you, even typing these words is hard for me.

I love my life today. I absolutely love each day. I'm the most fortunate, blessed person I know.

But in that moment, bound by that despair, the weight of it all overwhelmed me. I'm not sure I wanted to die, but I'm sure I didn't know if I wanted to live. I just couldn't see a way forward. It all felt so hopeless.

You don't need to experience something as dramatic as what I went through to feel utterly engulfed in despair. You have your own stories of relationships crumbling, friends letting you down, health failing, finances fleeting. You have your own experience of smoke rising from the things you hold dearest in your life.

You know life is hard.

You've been there, too.

You know life is made up of peaks and valleys and lots and lots of times of uncertainty, of living in between.

You also know that the painful moments can propel you forward or pull you back. They are inflection points creating the life you lead.

And you know that in these moments, having one person willing to be with you, to not let go of you, to speak truth to you, can make all the difference.

That one person for me was my sister Amy.

Hearing me say that I wanted to die, she pulled me even tighter. Amy then yelled at me something I welcome you to yell at me when we meet: "John, shut up. What's wrong with you? Listen to me, it's okay. Have faith and fight."

Awesome advice.

But difficult to live.

HOLDING ON

When life gets hard, we may want to give up.

But here's a secret that has gotten me through many a hard day, hard week, hard year:

When you know your why, you can endure any how.

I wish I could claim to have written that line. But I'll tell you about the man who first introduced it to me.

During World War II, Viktor Frankl spent years in Nazi captivity in Europe. Frankl was imprisoned in four different concentration camps in deplorable and inhumane conditions. Over three years, everyone he loved would perish. Everyone.

Frankl lost his parents, his brother, and his pregnant wife.

He lost neighbors and friends.

He was starved, beaten, and degraded.

He experienced pain I can't fathom.

Yet when he was released, he continued his psychology practice of helping others make sense of their lives. He also wrote an account of finding meaning and purpose in the midst of such intense suffering, *Man's Search for Meaning*. The book was originally titled *Nevertheless, Say Yes to Life: A Psychologist Experiences the Concentration Camps*. Did you know that? I mean, I love the current title, but something about the original is spot-on.

The book revolutionized psychology and cast a bright light on a tragedy many refused to discuss. It also dramatically impacted my life when I read it in college—and several times since.

And that phrase, *When you know your why, you can endure any how*, kept Viktor Frankl going through the unpardonable conditions, the starvation, the abuse by the Nazis, the death of friends, and the dread of waking up to the same nightmare every morning.

The morning he was captured by the Nazis, he had a book manuscript that he'd been working on in his pocket. When he arrived at the concentration camp, he was stripped of his clothes . . . and his precious manuscript.

Frankl knew that he would never recover all that hard work. That most likely it had turned to ashes moments after it was taken from him.

But he was determined to re-create that book. Throughout his time in captivity, he would write on scraps of paper. He would compose sections in his head. That book, that writing, became his why, and kept him going, striving to stay alive.

It was stunning he survived. And even once he was released, it would be understandable if that man wanted to say no to life. He saw the darkest of the dark. True evil. Unspeakable cruelty.

Yet he still chose to say yes to life. To find meaning. To find a way to overcome and keep going. To have faith and to fight.

We spend the vast majority of our efforts and life focused on the how. The how consists of the tasks, the duties, the obligations, the stuff, of life.

The how is car pools and social functions and work shifts. It's paying taxes and paying bills and paying for eating the irresistible dessert. It's strategy, it's the road map, it's the plan. It's a to-do list.

And it is always there.

Always wearing you down.

And so often, we forget why we are even doing it. We forget why we work, why we parent, why we serve, why we love, why we risk. Even why we strive to stay alive. It seems as if the bulk of life consists of the mundane; tasks that we must cross off every day.

Ah, but being on fire for life isn't about the *how*.

The chore may need to be done, the task may need to get accomplished, but everything about the chore, about the task, about *life*, changes when being lived out of the *why*. When the why is in front of you, reminding you of your purpose, every-thing changes.

When you know your why, you can endure any how.

Simple and powerful, Frankl's phrase reminds us of the importance of being on fire with purpose.

Because our why fuels us to tap into a reserve we'll need when times get hard.

Our purpose is the light that keeps us going through even the darkest tunnel.

It allows us to hold on tight, even when it burns, even when it's hard, even when it hurts like hell.

My siblings modeled this to me the day of the fire. After the ambulance drove away, my siblings were ushered into our neigh-bors' house and then late in the afternoon were brought to the hospital to be reunited with our parents.

Some staff shepherded Amy and my other siblings through the maze of hospital corridors. They took an elevator to the fourth floor. They stepped off and, directly in front of them, saw a waiting room overflowing with friends and family, gathered to support, cry, and pray with my parents.

Amy searched the room, found my dad, and ran to him.

They hugged.

She wept uncontrollably.

He held her tight.

Through faint whispers and sobs he listened to Amy share what she had seen that morning. She talked about the explosion, about seeing me in the hall, about the flames dancing from my body, about being outside, about being cold and scared, but also about knowing I needed her, about holding on to me.

"Daddy, John looked like he was going to crumble into ashes this morning. He felt so hot I thought I was burning my arms through my nightgown. But, Daddy, I never let go. I never let him go."

At a critical moment, when I wanted to die, she held on to me.

She refused to turn away.

She refused to let go.

She knew why she was in so much pain. She knew it was nothing compared to what I was going through. And she knew that if her embrace helped me, even if just a little bit, every ounce of pain was worth it for her.

When you know your why, you can endure any how.

She knew her why.

And so must we.

But it's crucial to realize that our greatest impact isn't just in the massive moments in life. Seldom are we called upon to become heroes during the tragic house fires of life. Much more frequently our purpose is required while living the seemingly routine, normal stuff of life.

A MASSIVE PAYCHECK

For my entire five-month interment, I lived in the burn unit.

Fourth floor.

Room 404.

Great view of a parking lot.

As is tradition in all hospitals, each morning the doctors performed rounds with the residents and a few frontline staff. My primary burn doctor, Dr. Ayvazian, would guide a group in white lab jackets through my room, talk about the treatment plan, and ask some questions. As a kid, I didn't like all the attention, so I normally just pretended to be asleep.

Just between you and me, I've been known to fall back into this defense mechanism when my wife asks me hard questions at night.

When are you going to change the light bulb above the front door?

Zzzzzz . . . zzzzzzz.

Should we go to your mother's or mine for Christmas?

Zzzzzz . . . zzzzzzz.

Do you like my hair better like it is or before I got my haircut?

Zzzzzz . . . zzzzzz.

Anyway, in one of those visits from all those staff members, the doctor asked one of the men to come forward.

It was Lavelle.

He was the janitor.

He would turn on the radio early in the morning and then clean my room. Since I was a kid, I didn't care how clean the room was. The only thing that mattered to me was Lavelle was cool. And he had great taste in music.

This particular day, Dr. Ayvazian had Lavelle come over to the side of my bed, looked him in the eyes, and said, "Take a good look at this little boy. You see him lying here? Lavelle, you are keeping him alive. You are doing this. This is the result of your good work. Thank you."

At the time, I didn't really know what the doctor was talking about. I didn't know that the number one killer of burn victims is infection. Infection kills in hospitals. And with no skin, it's highly likely that infection could have killed me. It's why my parents and brother had to cover their entire body head to toe in those yellow suits. They were designed to prevent germs from reaching me.

While the doctors did all they could to prevent infection, the most important person to diminish the likelihood of infection wasn't a doctor or a nurse.

It wasn't my parents or my brother.

It was the janitor.

A clean room was a safe room.

My doctor knew this. Even more, he knew the importance of purpose. Lavelle had many rooms to clean. Yet the doctor made him come on rounds. To remind him of something important.

All too often, we get caught up in the daily tasks. The humdrum. And when we do that, we can forget how important our efforts are in the greater scope of things. Every job undertaken, every task assigned, every responsibility assumed, does matter.

Do you believe that?

Do you believe that your work matters?

Your parenting matters?

The way you love your spouse matters?

The way you treat a stranger on the street matters?

Everything we do matters.

Our lives are sacred.

There are no small players.

There are no small tasks.

My medical team was exceptional. It was led by a doctor widely regarded as one of the best in the world. The nurses, respiratory therapists, pharmacists, dietitians, technicians, the entire staff all did their jobs flawlessly. Volunteers visited, the community prayed, but one mighty reason I survived was because of a janitor who was driven not by a task, but by a why. He was motivated not by a paycheck, but by a little boy's life.

All of it would have fallen apart if that man, one person, an ordinary person, chose not to care.

Indifference kills.

It kills patients. It kills relationships. It kills communities.

But purpose breathes life into others, into our work, into our relationships, and into our existence.

IGNITION STATEMENT

Do you have kids?

No?

Well, have you ever been around kids?

Good.

Think back to a time when they were about three years old.

Well, come to think of it, anytime from when they could first speak until whatever age they are today. What was their favorite question?

"Why?"

Whether it is "It's time to go to bed" or "Eat your vegetables" or "Put on a coat," kids follow up every statement with that inquisitive "Why?" It's cute for a while, but as parents you soon tire of answering every question, especially the tough ones you have no idea how to answer. *Dad, where do babies come from?*

But our kids are onto something.

When we understand the purpose of something, we can move forward clearly, without any nagging thoughts of *Is this worth it?* or *This is hard, there's no way I should be doing this.* When we know our why, it keeps us focused, on point, moving forward.

So how do you catch fire for life when the days get long and the going gets difficult and it feels easier to just quietly get by? To stop caring and let indifference take residence in your life?

You find a way to keep your why in front of you.

Several years ago I created a constant reminder to keep me motivated all day, every day, regardless of what I'm doing.

I call it my *Ignition Statement.*

Much like the mission statement that many organizations create, an Ignition Statement helps you determine what you are working toward every day, in good times and bad. The statement lights you up and reminds you what you are all about.

You see, your purpose acts like the fuel of your car. It keeps you going. If it starts to run low, you will find yourself running out of gas. An Ignition Statement is a constant reminder of what you are working for, whether at home, at work, or in your community. It can keep your tank full.

My traveling more than a hundred days of the year, supporting the growth of a business team, striving to impact lives, but at the same time longing to be home, desiring to be the best husband, father, and son that I can possibly be, could create tension. My Ignition Statement alleviates much of that tension by keeping me on fire when I'm on the road, at home, and everywhere in between. It helps to answer the question "Why do your absolute best and pour yourself into this situation with everything you have?"

For me, it's simple. My Ignition Statement took years of refining, but now it rolls off my tongue and through my actions: *Because God demands it, my family deserves it, and the world is starved for it.*

It lights me up going through security at the airport, greeting taxi drivers in new cities, speaking to audiences, hanging out with hotel staff, racing back to the airport, being kind to flight attendants and fellow passengers, and then being fully present with my beautiful wife and kids when I get home.

John, do you ever get tired?

Yes.

Are there days when you are physically in pain?

Absolutely.

Ever have days when you're just not up for it?

All the time.

So how do you keep going?

Easy.

Because God demands it, my family deserves it, and the world is starved for it.

Fires me up just thinking about it.

So let me ask you: Why are you here? Why do you want to thrive in life? Why give your absolute best and pour yourself into this situation with everything you have?

By answering these questions you begin to flush out your Ignition Statement. This statement should begin with *because*.

Because I matter.

Because this job counts.

Because my kids need me.

Because I love her, and I've got to show her, every day.

Because I'm healthy and alive and I want to make someone smile, even if it's only God.

Because it's worth it.

Because life is beautiful.

But let me be clear about something. Your Ignition Statement, the passion it unlocks and the purpose it fuels, is intended to inform and inspire your everyday life. It's not about taking the occasional mission trip or the first-class family vacation. It's not a focus on retirement in thirty years or your season tickets for next year. What I am trying to help you achieve here is the energy to keep you out of indifference while driving you forward with purpose in your everyday life.

The big trips matter. The planning for tomorrow is great. But real life takes place in the midst of diapers and car pools, spreadsheets and crammed calendars, rush-hour traffic and quiet evenings at home. It turns out that the mundane is the most sacred.

Your Ignition Statement reminds you to act like it.

GOING ALL IN

September 11, 2001, changed the world.

If you were alive at the time, you remember where you were and what you were doing when the planes went into the Twin Towers, the Pentagon, and the field in Shanksville, Pennsylvania.

Working a few miles from my parents' house, I raced home to watch the coverage and be with them. Mom and I sat on the couch, speechless, as smoke rose from the buildings.

We watched as battalion after battalion of youthful, vibrant, totally alive New York firefighters put on their jackets, grabbed their equipment, and made their way into the Towers.

Everyone else in the buildings did everything they could to get down, to get away, to leave the danger, to save themselves. And these heroes chose instead to walk right into it.

They weren't trying to become heroes. They didn't wake up hoping to become martyrs. Quite the opposite. They were compelled forward by love, by duty, by hope, by mission, by their *why*. They acted selflessly and saved lives while giving theirs.

They lived All In.

To truly be a hero, you've got to risk it all.

What are you willing to go All In for in life? What matters so much that you would risk everything else—your status, health, friendships, safety, even your very life?

Those who live passionate, effective lives know their answer to this.

They are transformed into heroes because they know their why.

Examples from this chapter include my brother, my sister, Lavelle, firefighters, and those in our armed forces. I want to introduce you to one more hero, one more individual who ran into the flames when everyone else was running out.

On the day I was burned, a little hero stepped forward and changed my life.

While flames continued leaping from our house, my sister Amy continued to hold and encourage me. As she told me that everything would be okay, everything would be fine, I repeated my request: *Go back into the house, get a knife, and kill me. It's not okay. It's not all right. Look at what I've done.*

Overhearing this life-and-death exchange was our younger sister, Susan.

She was eight, had pitch-black hair, big, puffy cheeks, an ever-present smile, and mischievous charm. I was her older brother. That means everything my older siblings did to me (think back to sandwiches laced with Tabasco sauce) that I hated them for, I would also learn from and then immediately do to Susan. Big families operate in much the same way as plumbing . . . they carry everything, *everything*, downstream.

Susan, come in here. I made you a peanut-butter-and-jelly sandwich. You'll love it!

So maybe it shouldn't have come as a surprise that when I stood in the front yard asking for a knife, little Susan didn't need to be asked twice.

This little girl left the safety and fresh air of the front yard. She turned and ran directly into our burning house. With the smoke wafting from the windows and doors, she entered the front hall. She worked her way through the family room. She made it all the way back into the kitchen.

She struggled seeing.

She had difficulty breathing.

But she knew the way.

And she knew the why.

Susan grabbed what she came in for and came sprinting back outside.

I'll never forget that moment when I stood in the front yard, held lovingly by Amy, watching our house burn, and saw my little sister sprinting out the front door.

It was like a movie.

She ran over to me, her face darkened, distorted with a grimace and tears and soot.

She stood two feet away from me.

Panting.

It was in her hands.

She lunged toward me with it.

And the cup of water she held went splashing directly into my face.

I wanted to die.

Susan had just risked her life for a cup of water—begging me to live.

After she threw the first cup in my face, she turned and ran directly back into the burning house. She made it back into the kitchen, filled a second cup with water, sprinted back outside, and threw it directly into my face.

She then turned and, on January 17, 1987, ran back into our house a third time.

In scripture, Jesus reminds us, "Greater love has no one than this: than to lay down one's life for one's friends."

At age eight she was willing to do this.

We think it's a miracle that she made it back outside with a third cup of water, throwing it directly into my face.

It made all the difference.

As you learned before, I had third-degree burns from my neck to my toes. My face and scalp, however, were not burned third-degree. Some credit Susan's actions in cooling my body in those areas for alleviating additional burning. They suggest Susan saved my scalp and face from also being burned third-degree. This is critical, because not only did her actions save my face, but also my scalp, which became the donor site for my entire body over the months of surgery and skin grafts to follow.

She saved my life.

It's a stunning, true example of being guided by a purpose bigger than any excuse.

It's a poignant reminder that when you know your *why*, you can indeed endure any *how*.

And it's an invitation to decipher what truly matters in our own lives so that we too can choose to go All In.

INDIFFERENCE V. PURPOSE

*A hero is an ordinary individual who finds the strength to
persevere and endure in spite of overwhelming odds.*
—Christopher Reeve

Are you on fire with purpose today?

I'm not asking when you last ran into a burning building or risked your
life for someone else. I want to know, are you living as if it matters? As if
something significant is at stake in your life today?

Are you All In?

Or have you allowed indifference to slowly steal all your joy? Are you
letting the mundane, the ordinary, the challenging, the boring, suck the
marrow from your life?

Let this be your inflection point.

Choosing to live on fire means you are unwilling to accept okay.

You can continue to retreat, protect yourself, disengage, and pretend not
to care. You can certainly cross your arms and say, "So what? I can't be
bothered. So what? I'm done caring. So what? It doesn't matter."

Or you can step back into the fight.

You can engage in the world around you, find your purpose, and cling
to it with all your might. You can proudly proclaim, "So what that it
sometimes burns? It's worth it. So what that I might get hurt? There are
other people that I can inspire. So what that it's hard? I've got one life
and I plan to never let go."

In choosing to be on fire with purpose you might just save a life.

Maybe even your own.

Choose purpose.

If you change the way you look at things,
the things you look at change.

—WAYNE DYER

4

WHY ARE YOU IN JAIL?

*Change the way you ask a question to transform the
answers you get—and the life you lead.*

*M*y eyes won't open.

I just went through another surgery.

My seventh.

By now, I know the drill.

They take me from my room in the morning.

Roll me downstairs.

*They all gather around me with their blue masks and little blue
hats.*

One of them puts a plastic mask on my face.

They talk to me about the weather or baseball or their families.

I fall asleep.

They do the surgery.

I wake up afterward, feeling groggy.

Supergroggy.

And always, always, the first people I see are my mom and dad. They're always there.

They feed me ice chips, congratulate me on getting through another surgery, and remind me we're one step closer to going home.

Sometimes they even have a new toy from the gift shop.

Most of my surgeries are performed to take skin from the one part of my body that was least burned, my head, to graft to the burned flesh on the rest of my body.

I don't understand how they do it, but they say they're patching me back together.

They're saying it's so I can go home.

And that's all I want.

I want to go home with Mom and Dad.

A nurse checks my vitals.

She talks to me, but I'm just too tired to look at her.

My eyes just won't stay open.

Then I hear a noise in the corner of my room where my parents usually are.

Hushed whispers. They're talking to each other.

I pry my eyes open again.

And see my mom crying.

What is going on? Why's she crying?

I never see my mom cry.

Mom doesn't cry.

Mom helps me when I cry.

She's always upbeat. Always positive. Always encouraging.

She's super-faith-filled—so seeing her tears makes me . . . scared.

My dad notices that my eyes are open.

He pats Mom's shoulder. She wipes the tears. She looks up with a smile.

They come over to my bedside and gently touch my shoulder.

"Hey, baby," Mom says. "How you feeling?"

I nod my head that I'm okay.

But I wonder what's wrong with them.

My dad steps forward.

He leans down.

His voice sounds a little strange . . . as if he's got a frog in his throat.

"John, we have to tell you something. This latest surgery went well. One more step closer to home . . . But, John, they . . . they had to remove your fingers. They were just too damaged by the fire, and they couldn't save them. Infection had set in and it was going to spread to . . ."

My dad keeps talking.

I stop listening.

What's he talking about?

I look down at my bandaged hands.

They look no different from before. Since I've been hospitalized, they've been covered with gauze.

They're still covered by gauze.

What does he mean I don't have fingers anymore?

I interrupt, "Will they grow back?"

He shakes his head. No.

I tell him fingernails grow back.

Toenails grow back.

Hair grows back.

How do you know that my fingers won't grow back?

"I'm sorry, John, they won't. They just won't."

My mind fast-forwards to life outside these walls.

Without fingers, I'll be unable to play baseball, write my name, go to school.

That means I can't get a job or earn money.

I'll be unable to have kids, a wife, and a life because what girl will ever want to hold hands with a boy without fingers?

I feel my body begin to shake, in rage, in shock.

How could you let them?

Dad, why did you let them do this to me!?

"John, we did it to save your life. We love you, more than ever."

I shake my head and lean back on the pillow.

I close my eyes.

I cry.

My life, I know, is over.

What's the difference between a tragedy and a triumph?

What separates a person who seems weighed down with continuous mishaps, playing out life like a tragedy, from someone who seems to experience difficulties, endures them heroically, and leads a life that reads like a tale of epic success?

Why do some people seem to repeatedly trip, fall, and fail their way through life, but others seem to bounce back, get stronger, and soar higher?

My friend, life is hard.

We all know that.

The storm of upheaval, challenge, and tragedy blows in all of our lives.

We've observed individuals endure difficulty and stay mired in the dirt. We know people who spend their entire lives trapped by disappointment, stuck in a rut, unable to bounce back, unable to move forward.

But we've also witnessed people rise from the ashes. We've seen individuals survive extraordinary trials and achieve astonishing success.

So what makes some people victims of circumstances and other people victors over them? Is it something within them, a hidden core of strength that you are either born with or without?

Nope.

The answer lies in how you ask one simple question.

THE VICTOR'S SHIFT

I have lots of heroes in my life.

You've met a few of them already. And as we continue, you'll meet more.

Heroes are important. They keep us focused on what is possible. They remind us of the power to overcome. They remind us what we know, deep down, is achievable. They remind us what we could do through our lives if we'd just stop making excuses. They remind us, too, that heroes seldom wear capes.

Some ordinary people decide to live extraordinarily, regardless of the difficulties they face. One of the best examples of this is my dad.

I imagine that for many kids their dad was their first hero. As kids, we look up to, revere, fear, and love our fathers. We want them on the sidelines when we're playing sports, we want to please them with our report cards, and we hope that they will be proud of us.

These days, it's Dad who is making me proud. He recently turned seventy, and for the past twenty-three years he has battled Parkinson's disease.

You're probably most familiar with Parkinson's disease thanks to the famous actor Michael J. Fox. He has remained in the public eye, and acting, despite all Parkinson's has taken from him. Parkinson's is a degenerative disorder that gradually impacts everything in your physical body. In time, Parkinson's rips away one's ability to type, write, drive, walk, speak, and eat. As a result, it becomes increasingly difficult to socialize. To work. To pursue hobbies. To function as a normal person.

To live.

Up until his diagnosis, Dad was tremendously industrious. He never missed a day of grade school, high school, college, law school, or work. (I used to miss school days on the chance that I *might* get sick.)

He prided himself on helping out around the house and in the yard (despite that his work both as a gardener and a handyman was a bit shoddy . . . sorry, Dad, it's true!).

He was always the first one up, the last one to bed, successful at work, present at home, in love with his bride, delighted in his kids, and active in his faith. He was the definition of a successful man.

It's been hard to see all of this health, energy, and vibrancy slowly drained from him. Dad can do little now physically, yet he is the most faithful, loving, and optimistic person I know. As obviously difficult as this disease is for Dad, it amazes me that I never hear him complain.

Now, when was the last time you complained?

Maybe the coffee shop forgot your cream?

Traffic was backed up?

The dry cleaner misplaced a shirt?

The steak was undercooked?

Many of us are experts at noticing what's wrong and complaining about it to others.

But I try to take lessons from my dad. Dad has braved this debilitating disease for more than two decades. He's fallen repeatedly, broken bones, endured surgeries, and takes medicine continuously. It's made his life extremely difficult and, lately, extremely painful.

And not once has he complained about it.

He's an amazing man.

When I grow up, I hope to be just like him.

With the amount of time I spend on the road for my speaking career, I relish my weekends at home. Many times I hunker down with my expanding and ever-active family at our house. The frenzied shouts and play of four little kids fill the rooms. We share waffles in the morning, sporting events throughout the day, and the occasional playdates with little friends.

Sometimes we unplug from the weekend sprint, pack up the car, and visit my parents. Mom can't get enough of her grandkids. Beth relishes another set of hands to wrangle the chaos. And I just enjoy visiting Mom and Dad.

On one such occasion Dad and I were sitting on his screened-in porch. Glasses of ice tea were on the coffee table in front of us. It was one of the more difficult days for Dad. He was clearly in pain. He wasn't able to get out of his wheelchair to greet us. Speaking was difficult for him. So we sat there in silence.

When you really know someone, you don't even need to speak to have a conversation.

But I had something I wanted to get off my chest. The day before I'd been speaking at an event and challenged the group to tell the heroes in their lives how they felt about them.

Sitting there next to Dad, I realized that maybe I should take my own advice. It's rare we get time together one-on-one. It's even rarer for me to share my heart.

My real heart.

So I looked over at Dad, and told him that I loved him. Told him he was an awesome dad. Told him I was proud of him.

He probably thought something was wrong with me and was getting ready to ask. *Are you sick? Have you been drinking? Are you moving? What's the deal?*

Rather than wait for his question, I continued, "Dad, I think of it every time I'm with you, but just wanted you to know it."

Though I was uncomfortable saying it, the smile on his face was a definite reward.

We hugged. He told me he loved me, too. He then took the occasion to tell me I was his favorite child. (No, he didn't! Dad often tells each of his six kids that he or she is his favorite . . . and he means it for each of us!)

We sat for a moment in silence. A weight had been removed from me. I'd shared something that had been in my heart, but never clearly verbalized. It was important for me to share and, judging by the beam in his eyes, important for him to hear.

"Dad, I know today isn't a good day for you. It seems things just keep getting harder. How is it that you stay so . . . well, positive?"

He nodded his head and smiled.

He took a sip of his ice tea, cleared his throat, and softly muttered, "Well, John, I don't know how I could be negative when I've got so much to be grateful for."

Dad said this while sitting in his wheelchair.

He was struggling to communicate.

He had already spilled one drink due to shaking.

He had a sling on his right arm from a recent fall.

Yet he said this sincerely with a smile on his face.

"Well, like what? How about this, Dad, can you tell me three things that you're grateful for because of Parkinson's?"

I knew Dad had a lot of blessings. But I was curious to find out how he made sense of such a terrible disease.

A serious but thoughtful look appeared on his face. "Well, first, I am grateful it wasn't a more serious disease."

I could barely understand him because his voice was so weak.

He took another sip of his drink, cleared his voice and continued.

"And I'm grateful for the time to reflect on who I am and who God is. I used to be so busy. I'm grateful for this time of reflection."

In a long pause before his third reply, he awkwardly moved his cup to his mouth and swallowed uneasily. "And, John, I've always liked your mom."

I chuckled. "Glad you like Mom, Dad. You've been married to her for forty-five years!"

"You're missing the point. This disease has chased some of my friends away. It's harder to do things. It's hard to get out of the house. It's even harder to get around the house. But your mom, my wife, just keeps stepping closer and closer. I love her. And I'm grateful for my relationship with her." He looked away from me and outside toward the garden.

I thought about his responses. Here is a disease that rips everything from the sufferer, yet he's grateful it wasn't worse.

This disease forces him into isolation, yet he's grateful for the time to reflect.

This disease makes him totally dependent on others, yet he's grateful for his relationships, specifically the one he shares with his wife.

I got up to give Dad another big hug. He faintly but firmly said, "John, sit down. I'm not finished. I've got more. Sit down.

"I'm grateful for medical technology, and those who provide it.

"I'm grateful for the empathy I've gained for others with challenges.

"When I can't walk or speak, I'm grateful for the days I can.

"When we drive, I'm grateful for the handicap spot.

"I'm grateful I was given the time to write my book, *Over-whelming Odds*.

"I'm grateful that each day I get to see, hear, learn, laugh, love, and live.

"And, John, I'm grateful for being healed, even if not cured. Parkinson's disease may end up killing me, but I get to wake up each day knowing that God has already healed me of it."

I had nothing to say in response. His answer left me speech-less.

All I could do was lift my glass in a salute, take a drink, try-ing to swallow down the lump in my throat, and look outside with tears in my eyes.

Dad's disease is what it is. We can't do much about it. But Dad owns the power for how he responds to it. This terrible dis-ease, his intense physical pain, his inability to earn a living and the resulting financial difficulties, have led to some of the greatest gifts in Dad's life—because he *chooses* to look for them.

He *chooses* to look for them.

He is a beautiful example of someone on fire for life. **And he exemplifies the fourth choice we face if we are going to live a radically inspired life. We choose to deliberately view life, all of life, the seemingly good and bad, as a gift.**

Because whatever we focus on in life grows.

Focus on the bad and it is multiplied, it's everywhere (watch the news tonight if you don't believe me. Reporters are experts at this). Focus on the good and it expands, it's all around.

Instead of looking at what he no longer has, my dad looks for what he does have.

Instead of looking for what is lacking, he looks for what he's blessed with.

We all know people who have everything and are grateful for nothing. We also know people who have nothing and are grateful for everything.

So which kind of person are you? And, more important, which kind are you going to be?

WHAT'S THE QUESTION?

I said earlier that the difference between a victim and a victor is how they ask one simple question. Let me explain.

What is the victim's favorite question?

Think about people you know who seem to always have the victim mentality . . . life is always battling against them, and they always have some drama to complain about. Whether they know it or not, they have a refrain playing over and over in their heads. They have a question they ask themselves and anyone else that might listen: Why me?

Why me? Why is this happening to me?

Why me? Why do things always go wrong for me?

Why me? Why does everyone else have good luck?

But you know what? Victors have a favorite question as well. A completely different question.

The question considers the cup not merely as half-full, but as running over. Victors ask a question that perceives the past as a wonderful teacher. They view the future as exceptionally bright. And they consider a challenge, whatever the challenge is, a gift.

The question victors ask themselves is . . . Why me?

Why did this happen to me? What lesson is it teaching? How can I conquer this circumstance, not allow it to drag me down, but allow it to raise me up and benefit others?

Why me? There must be some reason, something to learn.

Why me? No, things aren't perfect. But in the end they will certainly work out.

Why me? How did I end up in this place, with this life, and the amazing ability to do something with it?

Changing the way you ask this one simple question transforms the answers you get, what you do with them, and ultimately how you live.

The quality of our lives isn't a question of circumstances. The quality of our lives, the level of joy, and the ability to transform challenge into opportunity rests in our perspective.

Now, this isn't just "When life sends you lemons . . ." It's bigger than some motivational poster; it's better than some cheap bumper sticker.

How we choose to view daily events, personal relationships, chance encounters, and significant moments dramatically influences not only the life we live, but the longevity and vibrancy of it. This isn't just my opinion. Nope, some serious data backs this up.

In 1986, researchers at the University of Minnesota began an experiment that soon came to be known as the Nun Study. Nuns were considered a good population to study because, due to the strict regimen of their cloistered life, their lives had fewer variables than in the general population. Think about it—due to their vows, these women live similar lives, eat similar meals, work similar hours, under similar circumstances. In looking for a homogeneous group, this is about as good as it gets.

In the experiment, the researchers investigated and reviewed the journals and lives of 180 nuns from the Sisters of Notre Dame in Milwaukee. The researchers wondered if attitude and longevity in life were related. Sifting through the pages in the nuns' journals, the researchers tracked positive and negative comments. An entry such as "The food here stinks" was counted as negative. Conversely, "Grateful for another night of beans and rice!" was marked as positive.

So was there any connection?

Did it matter the way they asked the question *Why me?*

Did attitude impact longevity?

Did gratitude actually matter???

What do you think?

Careful research revealed that 34 percent of those who were least cheerful in their journaling were alive at age eighty-five.

Not bad.

Until you compare it to those who were most positive.

A stunning 90 percent of the nuns whose statements were most cheerful were still alive at age eighty-five. A decade later, 54 percent of the most cheerful were still alive at age ninety-four, compared to only 11 percent of the least cheerful. The numbers were staggering. The researchers looked for other factors that could explain this . . . how devout the nuns were, how intellectual, how active physically. But only one factor clearly predicted the length and vitality of life: the amount of positive or negative feelings expressed.

This is big.

Obviously we are all born with a particular temperament, and some people are naturally more upbeat and happy than others. But we can learn to incorporate gratitude in our lives. When life is getting us down and we start to hear the refrain *Why me? Poor me* playing in our heads, we can stop and recognize that moment as an inflection point. We can move forward with the same attitude, or we can actively try to turn it around.

We can take steps to overcome.

We can find reasons to be grateful.

But we must make that choice.

A LESSON LEARNED

I love the Christmas season.

The chilly weather, extensive family time, days off from work, delicious food, joyful music, church services, holiday decorations, Christmas lights . . . I love it all. And there is no better day during the season than Christmas Eve.

On December 24, 1998, as snow began to fall outside, my family gathered inside Mom and Dad's house. A fire crackled in the fireplace as they prepared for Christmas. Presents were wrapped, cookies were made, eggnog was consumed, and holiday cheer was spread.

Moments like this with family are long remembered.

Time together is so important.

Some things you just can't miss.

And I missed it.

Working as a college intern at a large financial firm in St. Louis, I spent my Christmas Eve shuffling papers under fluorescent lights. My productivity suffered mightily that day. In a pitiful trance, I stared out the windows, watched the snow fall, and longed to be with family.

But small heartaches can be wonderful teachers and motivators.

While sitting in my cubicle, I determined that this would be the last Christmas Eve I'd ever *have* to work. Not knowing what other business I could work for that assured me control of my schedule, I started my own. I considered starting a car wash or opening a coffee shop, but eventually settled on becoming a real estate developer.

For a guy who had never even painted his own bedroom, held a tool in his hands, or managed any significant project, this was a peculiar selection. A strange choice for a guy with no fingers. But it sounded fun and looked easy on TV.

So I bought some tools, and worked with a dear friend who had just embarked on a career as a real estate agent. Together we possessed a combined three weeks of experience, and so the search began to find the perfect fixer-upper.

In a matter of weeks, we purchased a 130-year-old, six-family structure in the heart of a historic neighborhood. We were thrilled. This was going to be easy, profitable, and fun. I could be my own boss, hire friends, control my schedule, and go to daytime baseball games. I could live the dream. What could possibly go wrong?

Everything.

It was a mess.

I distinctly remember my first day on the job. One of the electrical outlets wasn't working, so I assumed a circuit breaker was tripped in the basement. After finally finding the key to the lock to the basement, I got the door open and was greeted by darkness and a foul smell. With no lightbulbs working, I grabbed a flashlight and tiptoed down the decaying steps.

Remember when you were a kid and the basement was a scary place? Remember being terrified of it and not wanting to go down there? I mean, who knows what's really there?

Yeah, that's totally how I felt on this day.

Mustering up all my courage, I journeyed on, pointed the light to the bottom step, and saw three dead pigeons. Three freaking dead birds. I'm not cut out for dead birds. Stepping over them, off the final step and onto the floor, I realized I'd somehow missed something in the initial walk-through: the place had a dirt basement.

Maybe this was a sign.

If it was, I missed it.

After cleaning up those darn birds, I walked over to the electric panel, flipped the breakers back on, and got back to work.

And each day uncovered more challenges, bigger challenges.

The plumbing was corroded. The electric and HVAC needed a complete overhaul. The wooden floors that had attracted me in the first place were so damaged after years of abuse that they were unsalvageable. The roof leaked and many of the bricks on the outer walls were loose.

Despite working feverishly for a couple months I was making slow progress. Needing a little cheering up and free advice, I asked an older friend from church who actually *was* a developer to visit.

Dick arrived. Seeing his car pull up in the driveway out front, I came out the front door, struck a Superman pose, and got ready to give him a tour of my beautiful building.

He opened his car door, got out, took one glance at the building, and looked at me. "My God, John. Can you give it back?"

I don't think he was impressed.

The days were long and hot. The summer was stifling and there was no air-conditioning. My hands were rubbed raw, not accustomed to work of this sort. My ankles and feet were so irritated by my work boots rubbing against my scars that I'd have to wrap them in bandages each day before work.

Construction moved slowly.

The finances and time budgeted to the project were stunningly erroneous.

As the project neared completion, I hired an attorney to convert the apartments into individually salable condos. It was expensive. It was exhausting.

And it was, ultimately, a complete failure.

The units would not sell. Not at the price we expected. Not when we cut the price by 10 percent. Not when we slashed the prices by 20 percent. Nothing worked.

Eventually, I had to hire an attorney again, this time to convert the condos back into apartments for rent. The woman at city hall told me she'd never heard of anyone converting condos back to apartments.

Yeah, me either, lady.

I learned an awful lot about how not to make money in real estate during that difficult time. It humbled me, grounded me, almost broke me, but ultimately taught me vital lessons that would serve me well during my next decade of work as a developer.

Many times during this endeavor *Why me?* began to play in my head. *Why me? Couldn't just one thing go right in my life?*

But you know what?

In time, I was able to take that question, the one leading me down one path, and begin asking it differently. During the darkest, longest, hottest days working in that old oven of a building, I began to ask instead, *Why me? What is this preparing me for next?*

You see, gratitude leads not only toward a heart that is thankful for what you have, but grants you the courage and determination to move through any adversity you face.

In my old, beat-up, white Ford F-250 I had a quote taped above my visor:

Gratitude unlocks the fullness of life. It turns what we have into enough, and more. It turns denial into acceptance, chaos to order, confusion to clarity. It can turn a meal into a feast, a house into a home, a stranger into a friend. Gratitude makes sense of our past, brings peace for today, and creates a vision for tomorrow.

—Melody Beattie

On many early mornings in that truck I needed the reminder.

And countless times since, I've leaned back into the truth of this quote.

In my faith life, when the storms have blown, when I've had

doubts, I've found it so liberating to look up, arms in the air, and in prayer request the answer to *Why me?*

The question asked, though, not as one who is a victim, but with the sincere, heartfelt realization of the innumerable gifts I've already received, and those that I know deep down are on the way.

THE NUMBER ONE JOY INDICATOR

I recently had the opportunity to speak at a leadership event for one of my absolute favorite companies, Southwest Airlines. Also invited to present was one of my favorite speakers, Brené Brown. In the last five years, she has become one of the world's leading experts on vulnerability, courage, and leading an authentic life.

What stuck out to me the most during her talk was this:

"The number one joy indicator, the one thing that will predict whether someone feels joy in their life or not, is the practice of gratitude." This is not her opinion. She has been studying this stuff for twelve years.

Her research shows that joy is not a question of what happens to you, how much money you have in the bank, your looks, your kids, or the vacations you're able to afford. It's about actively choosing to practice . . . gratitude. As she writes in her book *Daring Greatly*, "In fact, every participant who spoke about the ability to stay open to joy also talked about the importance of practicing gratitude. This pattern of association was so thoroughly prevalent in the data that I made a commitment as a researcher not to talk about joy without talking about gratitude."

You can't have joy without gratitude.

But what surprised her in her research was that the things that people were the most grateful for were the ordinary things in life. The sound of your spouse's laugh, the smell of morning coffee, the echo of children playing in the yard. The little things.

In waiting for the big moments—the vacations, the retirements, the birthdays—we risk missing the experiences of life most worthy of celebrating.

I'm grateful that I am now paying attention and celebrating the little things. I now understand that there are no "ordinary" moments. It's all a gift, all a miracle. The habit began several years ago after I visited a friend's father in the hospital. He had abdominal cancer, and the growth had become so intrusive that he was unable to use the restroom anymore.

Near the end of our visit he said, "John, if I ever go to the bathroom again, I'm going to have a flippin' party. The patients two floors down will hear me doing my happy dance up here. It's going to be a party—and everybody will be invited to party with me!"

I'm writing this almost five years after that conversation, the last I had with this great man. In the five years since, I've tried to give thanks all day for everything.

The good and the bad.

The big and the little.

Yes, even every time I use the restroom, I do a little happy dance. It freaks people out in public restrooms, but serves as a great conversation starter.

I do it in part to honor my friend. But also because once you see those who have lost the ability to do what we all take for granted so much of the time, you realize how much of a gift those things actually are.

BREAKING DOWN THE WALLS

A few years ago, I was asked to speak at a federal prison.

It was my first time in a jail. I wasn't sure what to expect.

I was nervous.

The massive anxiety only increased as I drove toward it. A sign on the entrance highway read DO NOT PICK UP HITCH-HIKERS. In front of every parking spot was a second sign: LEAVE EVERYTHING IN THE CAR. BRING NOTHING IN.

Without my cell phone, car keys, laptop, and wallet, I made my way up the steps and into the penitentiary. A buzzer sounded and I was granted access into the waiting area. A guard had me sign in, verified information, and provided instructions on what to do if any unexpected flare-ups occurred among the men.

The guard led me down a short, darkened hallway, to another metal door.

It buzzed, and slowly opened.

I walked in.

It was a small holding area, metal and concrete on four sides, with a video camera above. As a security precaution, the door to the prison grounds can't open until the door to the outside world, the one I'd just walked through, has shut.

My heart pounded.

I waited for the next door to open, the one to the prison courtyard.

I was about to join the prison population and provide a workshop on leadership.

All 147 pounds of me.

I've spoken to groups around the world, from executive teams of Fortune 500 companies to sales rallies for more than fifteen thousand insurance agents. I've never been as nervous as that afternoon.

Finally, the last large, metal door buzzed open.

I took a step forward. The door slammed behind me. A gentleman greeted me, shook my hand, and briskly walked me toward the session.

The common area was loud. It sounded like a park—with laughing and cussing and talking. Dozens of men to my left were on the grounds playing basketball, running track, working out, playing chess, or standing idly.

We walked past them, to a door marked *8* and into an old chapel. The room was hot and dimly lit, with a single fan charged with creating a breeze.

In the room sat sixty men in orange jumpsuits.

There was no official introduction. I was told that when I was ready, I could begin speaking.

I gathered my thoughts, said a prayer, looked around the room. And began to talk. I figured I should start with the truth. I shared how I felt pulling up, seeing the signs, walking through the July sun, up the steps, and to the front door. I told them I was petrified waiting for that final door to open that would expose me to the general population. I told them I'd had second thoughts about coming.

And I told them that right now, in this room, there wasn't a place in the world I'd rather be.

We spent three hours together. I shared with them lessons that had allowed me to endure the months spent locked in my hospital room and the freedom the lessons provided then—and today—to live beyond perceived walls. We shared stories, discussed overcoming challenges, and considered strategies to discover meaning and hope and forgiveness even within those four walls.

Nearing the end of our time, the value of gratitude came up. An old piano was in the chapel. I sat down at the piano and began to play "Amazing Grace." People are always astonished that I can play the piano without fingers. I like to play at night to relax, but I sometimes play at presentations to encourage others. On this day, I thought the quiet music might help get these men in a reflective state of mind.

I thought about the conversation I'd had with my dad just a few weeks earlier and decided to use the same tactic here.

"I want you men to think of three things that you are thankful for. More specifically, three things you are grateful for because of your time in prison."

I heard some soft laughter and murmurs throughout the room. No big deal. I knew this might be a tough exercise.

I didn't respond.

Just kept playing.

After a few more minutes, I stopped playing, stood up, and asked:

Who wants to share?

Heads went down.

No one said a word.

Crickets.

Finally, I heard someone clear his throat.

He put his hand in the air.

I nodded at him and thanked him.

He stood.

Looked around at the guys in the room. Then stared at me.

Then shared, "Not one goddamn thing."

He sat back down.

The room erupted in laughter.

The question *Why me?* began to dance through my mind!

I thanked him for sharing and asked if anyone else had something on his list.

More silence.

Finally, a folding chair scraped against the tile floor.

A man toward the back of the room stood up.

"Well, sir"—the voice was clear and strong, with the man staring at the floor, his raggedy, rust-colored mustache covering up his mouth as he spoke—"I'll share. Here we go. . . ." He looked at the list he'd been making and began sharing.

And sharing.

He listed thirty-one things he was thankful for.

Heat in the winter. Air-conditioning in the summer. The library. A warm bed. Laundry service. A chance for redemption. New friends. Leaving behind old circumstances. Three square meals daily. A bed. A pillow. A blanket. Life.

He sat back down.

No one moved. The room was momentarily hushed.

Then the chapel erupted in applause.

It was absolutely magical.

When the first man had sat down, everyone laughed at him.

When this gentleman sat down, the others leaped to their feet, giving him a standing ovation.

Same walls.

Same orange jumpsuit.

Same time.

Same meals.

Same experience.

Same question.

But changing the way you ask the question transforms your answer, alters your daily experience, elevates your life, and inspires others.

"IT'S YOUR CHOICE"

With just a few days left before I was to be released from the hospital, there was a knock at my door.

It was Dr. Ayvazian.

He had greeted me in the emergency room months earlier. He had been with me through the five months, the two dozen surgeries, and the daily procedures. Besides my parents, he was the one person I saw every single day during my time in the hospital.

Even though I was still angry that he'd taken my fingers, I loved Dr. Ayvazian.

He was short, wore glasses, was always smiling, had a twinkle in his eye, and spoke to me as if he understood what I was going through.

And he did.

You see, as a child he was in a fire. He had scars all over his legs. Because he always wore dark suit pants, I never saw them, but you don't need to see scars on people to know they've been burned. You can see it in their eyes. You can hear it in their voices. You can feel it in their compassion. This man understood. He was incredibly empathetic, friendly, and a world-class surgeon. He would end every visit by saying, "Good-bye for now, my little comrade."

I never told him, or asked anyone else, but as a kid I had no idea what a "comrade" was. The only time I'd heard the word was in movies. Usually the person saying it was Russian. *Little comrade," huh? Okay. Um, is that good or bad?*

I didn't know.

So I'd just nod and say, "Okay."

On this visit, a week before I was going home, he came into my room in the middle of the afternoon. He turned off my television, sat on the bed, and smiled at me. "John"—his eyes shone with emotion—"your recovery is miraculous. I have never seen anything like it in my entire career. I am so glad that you've had the support of your friends and family, and their many prayers that have gotten you to this day."

He paused.

"But, as difficult as the past four months have been, the journey forward will be equally as challenging."

I nodded. I knew what he had to say was important. Even as a kid, you know. I also knew that he was sharing this because he had walked the road himself.

He cleared his throat. "John, do you know that you can still do almost anything you want in your life? Perhaps you won't be a court reporter, but you can be a lawyer or a judge. You may not play baseball again, but you can be a manager or own a team. You may not be able to be a carpenter, but you can be a general contractor and build incredible things. John, if you want to get married and raise kids and have an incredible life, you can! You are a remarkable little boy; you can still live an amazing life. You've endured something terrible, but the best is yet to come. The way I see it is, you can either be a victim to this tragedy or you can rise above it and be a victor. It's your choice."

Again, I nodded.

He bent down and kissed me on my forehead.

He stood, walked away from the bed, slid open the door to leave the room, then turned back. "Good-bye for now, my little comrade."

Those words, that visit, have stuck with me for almost thirty years. I know he was a busy man. He could have just crossed me off his list. I was being released; his work was done.

But he wanted to do more. He wanted to express to me that I could choose to look at what I could no longer do, or I could see the opportunities that were still available.

Without people to show us what is possible, we can forget the power we all hold to make an incredible life.

This man was an exceptional leader of his staff. He worked round the clock on my care. He was supremely dedicated to all of his patients. He also cared enough to ensure that we not only would be pushed out of the hospital, but might someday walk boldly back into life.

The victor's shift means we immediately look to what we have, not what we lack. With gratitude, we unlock vitality, longevity, and optimism. We escape from chains that bind and walls that trap into a life that is on fire and a party that is raging.

The kind of party where patients two floors down will hear us doing our happy dance.

The kind of party that sparks a standing ovation from fellow inmates.

The kind of party that ignites a radically inspired life.

Let the dancing begin.

VICTIM V. VICTOR

Life isn't about waiting for the storm to pass, it's about learning to dance in the rain.
—Vivian Greene

Why me?

A simple question.

With profoundly important consequences.

Storms will always rage. As a victim we stare up at the sky, lift our hands in despair, and cry, "Why me?" We realize clearly that our life is a struggle, that others are evil, that there is no hope, and that the worst days are to come.

Or we choose another way.

In the middle of the same storm, we can choose to be a victor. To recognize that a disease is a gift, the walls can't contain our spirit, the fire has refined and strengthened our character, and the best days are in front of us. We lift our hands, feel the rain on our face, and dance. *Why me?* We know this is leading us somewhere. We know that this storm isn't the end. We're just waiting for the first sunbeam.

Why me?

The manner in which we ask this question changes everything that happens afterward.

Choose wisely.

Choose to be a victor.

No matter how bad life may seem,
if there is life there is hope.

—STEPHEN HAWKING

5

CAN YOU SAY YES?

Comfort is popular, but courage changes lives.

*H*ere he comes again.

He's been around for as long as I've been here. He's the guy in charge of my bandage change. He's the one who gets me out of bed, on a gurney, down the hall, to the tub, and back.

He's a huge guy. He looks just like Apollo Creed. You know, the big boxer who fights Rocky? Yeah, when he's not fighting Rocky, he's working here. I call him Big Roy.

And he used to be my favorite nurse.

He used to be the one I'd ask for because he was so gentle. He was the best at carefully getting me out of bed, rolling me to the bathtub, and tenderly setting me in it.

He used to be the best.

But now he's the worst.

He changed.

I'm not sure why.

The past few days he still comes into my room, but he hasn't been putting me on a gurney.

Instead he comes in, unstraps the Velcro that fastens me to the bed, picks me up, holds me upright, and tries to make me walk to the bandage-change room.

My legs dangle between his.

Doesn't he know I can't walk? Doesn't he know my legs don't work?

My feet don't even touch the floor.

But my feet and legs throb like heck. All the blood races down to them. It causes a huge burning in my legs. I tell him to put me down. To roll me back. I tell him it hurts. I tell him to stop.

Instead of listening, he gets mean about it.

My legs drag on the floor between his, and he says to me, "Boy, you are going to walk again. You might as well get used to it. Come on, I'll walk with you."

Seriously. Can you believe that?

I mean, what is he thinking?

My legs are still completely wrapped in bandages. And what's underneath those bandages is a mess.

I can't bend my legs. I can't put weight on my feet. I have no muscles.

I am not going to walk again.

And I'm ok with it.

Mom and Dad will take care of me. My sisters will help, too.

I don't need to walk again. Or do anything again. I'll be fine just like I am.

And now he's in my room again.

He unfastens my right arm. Then my left.

He unstraps my left leg. Then my right.

He gently picks me up; he carries me out of the room. And then he does it again.

He lowers my legs to the floor. My feet barely touch the floor. He bear hugs me. He starts moving me toward the bandage change room. My legs swing lifelessly between his.

And then he starts talking to me.

"Boy, listen to me: you are going to walk again. You might as well get used to it. Come on, move those legs. There you go. Boy, come on, I'll walk with you."

I try to ignore him and ignore the pain he's causing.

I stare down at the floor.

Whatever, Roy.

I'm not going to walk again.

An old pickup truck pulled up our driveway.

I'd been waiting for this moment, for this truck, and for the man driving it. I watched from a chair in the front hall as an old man stepped out. He shut the truck door, pivoted around, and walked toward our house.

It was late winter, about a year since I'd been burned. Although I was finally out of a wheelchair, my body was hunched forward, my arms were stuck at ninety degrees, splints still adorned my arms, neck, and legs, and I walked with a bad limp. The ongoing physical therapy was painful and its impact slow. Sure, I was "walking," but not like normal. Now that I was out of the hospital, I was desperate to be a normal kid again. To run. Play baseball. Shoot baskets. Keep up with the other kids. It was taking too long and I was discouraged.

Then a gentleman called my parents. He'd heard about my story and wanted to pay me a visit. He wanted to take a walk with me. One-on-one. Man-to-man.

That's all I knew as I opened the door for him. We introduced ourselves in the front hall, my parents told us to enjoy our time, and the two of us "men" hobbled outside. Our gaits were similar, his due to age, mine due to the scarring that covered my entire body.

And this old man told me his story.

His name was Glenn Cunningham.

He asked if I knew anything about him.

I shook my head no.

So he told me a little bit about himself.

In his youth he was an all-American athlete. At one point he held the world record for the fastest mile ever run. As an Olympic runner he won a silver medal in the 1936 Olympics.

He stopped and turned toward me.

"You know what, though? You and I, John, we're not so different. When I was a little boy, I got burned in a fire, too. I was trying to start the stove in our schoolhouse with my older brother. It was cold and we were the first ones to school that day. We wanted to get the stove burning so the room would be warm when others got there for class. John, we had no idea that the night before they'd switched the kerosene can with gasoline. That's not good, is it?"

I shook my head. *No, sir. Not good at all.*

"John, that morning, in that school, next to the burning stove, the can ignited. Everything was on fire. The entire room just . . . it just turned to flame."

He paused and looked away.

"My older brother, Floyd, was my best friend. He was part of every childhood memory I had, and he was with me in that schoolhouse that morning. He died nine days after the fire."

Seven decades later the pain of that loss could still be clearly heard in Glenn's voice; the heartache still reflected in his eyes. Time had not healed these wounds.

"John, I was burned all over. Even though I was grateful to be alive, the pain was so intense that sometimes I wanted to die. You know what I mean?"

I didn't respond right away. We took a few more steps. Eventually, I looked up at him and quietly answered.

Yes. I do.

We continued to slowly make our way down the sidewalk.

"My entire body was burned, but my legs were burned the worst. The doctor wanted to amputate them because they were burned so badly. If they got infected, it was certain death. Luckily my mom begged the doctor to save them, promised she'd do all the bandage changes, every day, as long as I had a chance to learn to walk again."

He paused again. "It took a long time, John. It took a long time to get out of bed. It took a long time before I could stand, before I could walk, before I could even think about running."

How did you do it?

"At first my mom would carry me out of the house and stand me next to the fence that circled our property. I'd just hold on to it until I fell down. Get up, hold on longer, and fall down again. Then she'd carry me back in the house. After a while, I'd hobble out of our house all by myself. I'd get to the fence and hold on to that darn fence with both hands and slowly make my way along it, step-by-step around the farm. Eventually, I was able to walk along holding on with only one hand. Then no hands! I started walking next to it, then jogging next to it, and eventually sprinting next to it. I got faster. Could go further. Then I started running races. I didn't think I'd end up at the Olympics. All I knew was, I wasn't going to live my life sitting down. So I got up. I put one foot in front of the other. And I never looked back and never quit. Not on that farm. Not running in college. Not racing in the Berlin Olympics."

Glenn turned toward me and bent down awkwardly so he could look me in the eye. His voice was strong and determined.

"John, I didn't drive all the way here to talk about me. I'm here because I believe in you. I've heard what you went through—and I know what you're going through now. It's a fight. It's a struggle each day. But think back about how far you've come since your first day in the hospital. People didn't think you would live through the night! And here you are, proving them wrong!"

I nodded.

"You've come so far, John. And you are just beginning. Just picture yourself doing whatever you desire to do. Visualize it. Don't be satisfied with mediocrity. You will be able to do whatever you believe you can do. Set high goals and expect high achievement. Don't give in when it gets hard. Don't ever give up on your dreams. That's the key: never give up."

We walked back to my house with Glenn asking questions and offering encouragement.

I needed Glenn in that moment. I needed to know someone else had walked this same path. As a ten-year-old kid, walking around with an Olympic medalist and burn survivor transformed the way I felt about my current situation. It was the first time I really believed that if he could do it, so could I.

When it was time for him to leave, I walked Glenn from the porch to his red pickup truck. It took a few tries, but eventually the engine revved to life. He rolled down the window, put his head out, waved, and yelled as he pulled away, "John, never quit!"

It was an incredible conversation.

It changed my life.

And it almost didn't happen.

Just two weeks after Glenn pulled out of my driveway, he died at his home in Arkansas. He was seventy-eight. A man who'd spent his life overcoming odds and generously investing in others had delivered one last gift, a gleam of hope for an impressionable little boy still learning to walk.

Glenn's visit occurred more than a year after the voice of Nurse Roy first prodded me forward, his deep voice echoing in my ear and tickling hope in my heart. "Boy, you are going to walk again. I'll walk with you."

Roy's visits were needed, too. As much as I hated him at first, didn't believe it was possible, and disliked the pain from those walks to the tub, one day everything changed. One day on our walk back to the bandage change I believed. One day I bought in to what he was trying to do. *Maybe, just maybe, I will do this. I will walk again.*

Sometimes we need others to walk with us, imagine what's possible through our lives.

I wouldn't be who I am today without Glenn and Roy. These two men met me where I was, but refused to allow me to keep my eyes down on present challenges. They cheered me forward, pointing me toward where I could go. They cast a mighty, daring vision. They believed before I did.

These two men taught me something transformative.

They showed me the power of looking up.

LEARNING TO FLY

I love coming home from work.

A few weeks ago, pulling into my driveway, I was greeted at my car by three of my kids, Jack, Patrick, and Grace. I gave out hugs, played a quick game of tag, then went inside to find Henry and my wife.

Beth was getting dinner ready. We kissed hello, talked a bit about our days and about the evening ahead. She then asked me to get the kids inside for dinner. Still not seeing Henry, I stepped into the foyer and called out his name. No reply.

He's only four so I started getting a little anxious.

I climbed the stairs calling his name.

Still no reply.

I got to the top of the steps, reaching our family room, which sits high above the backyard. It has windows on three sides and a beautiful panoramic view. And tonight, from on top of the back of our couch, forehead pressed against those windows, stood a little boy wearing a Teenage Mutant Ninja Turtle mask and Superman cape with a light saber in his right hand.

He turned and waved the light saber at me with menace.

The week before we'd been to the ER for stitches for this little man. It was not his first time there. From deep, gaping cuts on his hands to a quarter in his stomach, we've gotten to know the nurses at the ER well over the past few years. Not wanting to visit our friends again I snapped:

Henry, put down the light saber and get off the couch, little man! If you fall out the window, you'll find out quick that you can't fly. Get down, Hen!

He jumped down, ran over to me, and attacked me with karate chops and hugs. His love gave me pause, softened my heart, and reminded me that it wouldn't be long before he actually believed those words I spoke.

It wouldn't be long before he lowered the light saber and threw it away for good. Before he thought, *There's no such thing as superheroes.*

It wouldn't be long before he took off the cape, stepped down from the couch, walked to his room, stuffed the cape in a corner of his closet, and thought, *That's all just pretend. Kid stuff.*

In other words, it wouldn't be long until the massive playfulness, creativity, and wild hope for each moment got sucked out of him. Soon, he'd be like the rest of us. Shirt tucked in. Left foot in front of the right. Living like everyone else. Believing that a wildly exciting, joy-filled life, where anything is possible, was impossible.

I just wanted, as a parent, to keep Henry safe. But when we try to stay safe, when we strive to stay comfortable, we miss the great opportunities of life.

We all face moments when we would rather stay where we are. Whether we are too injured, or it's too late, or it's too scary, those excuses arise because we have been trained to keep our eyes down, on the rocky soil in front of us, trying to make sure we don't trip. *We've got to stay safe,* we think. *Looking down is just practical. Don't want to look stupid. Don't want to fall.*

But when we are staring down at where we are, we can't look ahead at where we could go. We miss the beauty of what's possible. And we certainly can't see the path to get there.

What we need is a return to the mind-set that whispers to us, "Anything is possible." What we need is the courage to go back to the drawer where we tucked away our cape. You know, the one you used to wear when you were little, when life was full of limitless potential? We need to find the courage to put that cape back on. To look up at the horizon. To climb back onto the couch. And to dare to fly.

It's time to dare again.

It might be painful.

But it will totally be worth it.

LESSONS FROM THE BROOM CLOSET

For five months I was strapped to a hospital bed.

During those months of fighting just to survive the fire, my muscles atrophied and I had no muscle mass left. In addition to the lack of muscle, the skin grafted onto my body was saving my life, but also presenting another challenge. The postage-stamp-size skin grafts taken from my scalp were strategically placed to cover the areas of my body where the skin had completely burned off. This new growth of skin came with a new hurdle: scarring. Thick scars began to tug on my joints. This was why my body was strapped down to the bed in an X position with my arms and legs fully extended. If the skin contracted, it meant limited mobility or a slow retreat to a fetal position.

To prevent this, I needed stretching. I needed physical therapy.

Every day, Maureen and Brenda would appear in my room, unfasten me from the bed, unhook the machines, and set me in a wheelchair. They'd roll me out of the room, out of the burn unit, down the hallway, to the elevators. They'd hit the button marked *B* and we'd descend to the basement. Never a good sign.

They'd roll me into a large physical-therapy room, gently pick me up, and set me on a yellow mat. Surrounded by a bunch of other patients, they'd begin to slowly stretch every joint on my body. Usually beginning with my ankles and toes, they'd aim to put as much movement back into my joints as they could.

They'd work on each joint for a few minutes.

Take a short break.

Bend it in the opposite direction.

Take a short break.

Then move on to the next joint. Then the next. Ankles. Hips. Arms. Legs. The entire body.

Then they'd flip me over and start stretching everything again.

It was torturous.

After forty-five minutes it was time for a break. They picked my limp body up off the mat and set me back in the wheelchair. They rolled me down a hallway, made a left-hand turn, opened a door, and pushed me inside. The room was full of mops and buckets and brooms and cleaning supplies.

It was the janitorial broom closet.

You see, they were about to embark on the toughest part of my therapy: bending my knees. If I was ever going to walk again, my knees would have to bend. Right now they were locked in place.

These therapists took me to the broom closet out of respect for me (and the other patients). They wanted me to be able to cry out in pain. And they didn't want to scare anyone else.

We had a routine. Maureen would walk over to me, put a towel in my mouth so I'd have something to bite into. She'd lock the wheelchair brakes. She'd hold me down at my hips. Then the other therapist, Brenda, would come toward me, bend down, and start working on my knees.

I've had hernias, broken bones, burns, bandage changes, infected abscesses, and cellulitis. I've had fingers amputated, joints stretched, blood drawn from my toes, and skin grafted from my head. I've endured about every kind of physical pain outside of natural childbirth—and my wife says if I want a fifth child, I'll have to personally go through that one, too. But this therapy was the most acutely painful experience of my life.

These therapists were stretching skin that had grown taut; it was not flexing. They were stretching joints that had begun to permanently harden into position. They were stretching a little boy who, despite the towel in his mouth, was weeping and screaming and begging them to stop.

I remember looking down through my tears at them. I remember seeing my pain reflected on their faces. I remember seeing tears in their eyes. And I remember thinking, *What are you crying about? I'm the one being tortured!*

Oh, how amazing those therapists were in my recovery.

I live an incredibly active life today, and many individuals deserve an awful lot of credit for that. But no one more than those therapists, in that basement, in that darn broom closet, stretching through their personal anguish of watching a little boy in pain so that they might liberate him from the scars that bound him.

It makes me emotional decades later just thinking about them.

How did they do it?

Why not take the easier way?

Why not stop when the little boy said, "Ouch!"

These therapists knew that stretching is never easy. It's unwanted. It's painful. It's hard on all parties involved and in all facets of life. It's not pleasant to be stretched and it's not pleasurable to stretch others. Yet the pain of today unveils the possibility of tomorrow.

Stretching leads to growth.

Growth is frequently painful.

But "growth is the only evidence of life."

John Henry Newman was a wise theologian, incredible thinker, and prolific writer. That is one of his most remarkable quotes. Think about it. Growth is all about new beginnings, a different direction, a budding relationship, a big move, that new position, a bold conversation, the daring venture, the next chapter in your life.

Growth is the only evidence of life.

The opposite is true, too. Stagnation is the first step to your grave.

You ready for number five?

The fifth choice that you must make to live a radically inspired life is this: refuse to become stagnant by purposefully growing and intentionally stretching in every area of life.

When a couple stop actively dating, stop pursuing one another, stop choosing to really love, stop choosing to grow together, stop choosing to continually forgive—they begin to die. They didn't fall out of love. They stopped growing in love.

When an organization stops innovating, stops doing things differently, stops investing in its people, and stops dreaming big, it stops growing and begins to die.

When we stop paying attention to our health, when we make poor choices in our diet or addictions or exercise, we have chosen to be comfortable, to stop growing, to slowly recede. These choices lead away from health and vitality. And though the slope may be imperceptibly slight, they lead in time toward illness and death.

Death seldom occurs overnight. It's a slow fade. The changes can be subtle, but make no mistake: in choosing not to grow, we choose to die.

In today's culture when things get uncomfortable, we often see it as a sign that something's wrong.

But I know personally that we've got to learn to see discomfort differently. It may be a sign that something is *right*. It may be proof that we are growing in a new direction. The poor kid with a towel in his mouth would have remained locked in bed unable to walk had it not been for Brenda and Maureen, for the broom closet.

It's not just those enduring physical therapy who benefit from being stretched. You've likely made the greatest advances in your life when you were made uncomfortable. Think of your best teachers in school. They likely were dynamic, but the reason you learned the most is they made you work. Things that come easy are seldom worthy. Stretching forward may not be fun, but it may possibly be something much more significant: life-giving.

Real growth is often unwanted, extremely painful, and ultimately completely worth it.

GET YOUR GROW ON

Man, life was getting good.

Seven years into my career as a real estate developer, I was finally figuring out how to actually do this work. I could plan a job, run a crew, and even make a little money. I was finally getting comfortable.

My crew was rehabbing a historic multifamily structure. The blueprints of the building were unfurled on the hood of my truck. My loyal foreman, Harold, and I were going through the plans and making a list of required materials for the following day.

My phone rang.

It was a woman who led a third-grade Girl Scout troop. She and her daughter had read my parents' book, *Overwhelming Odds*. They were both deeply moved by the story, and she asked if I'd be willing to share my story with their troop.

I walked away from Harold to the back of the truck.

There was a long, awkward silence.

You mean, like, you want me to speak to the girls?

"Exactly. We'll get the girls together after school, have snacks, you can speak, and the girls will ask some questions. How about next Wednesday?"

More silence.

By now, you probably know what this moment was.

That phone call was an inflection point in my life.

It seemed like a minor one at the time; a simple yes or no to her request. But as you read on, you will see how huge it really was. It changed the rest of my life.

I try to say yes as frequently as I can to new possibilities. Yes to serving. Yes to making a difference. Yes to new foods, new things, new people, and new ideas. When you say and live yes, greater possibilities open each day than you could have imagined.

But every bone in my body was crying out for me to say no.

I looked down at my feet. Stared at the dirt.

Then looked up. I saw my building, then the beautiful trees, and then a brilliantly blue sky.

Took a deep breath and murmured, *Yes. Sure. I'll do it. Sounds perfect.*

We agreed on a time, she gave me directions, and we ended the call.

I stared back at the building, back toward my truck, back at Harold, and said aloud, "Oh, crap. What did I just do?!"

Yes, my parents' book was in circulation, but I'd still never really told anyone the story. I'd still not told close friends from grade school, high school, or college. Not the guys I worked construction with every day. Even my wife and I had seldom discussed the fire. She'd read the book, wept like a baby, and couldn't believe all we went through, but we didn't harp on it. It happened in the past. It was over. It didn't define us. Our life was good.

And now I'd have to figure out a way to share my story with a bunch of little girls . . . and I didn't have the first idea where to begin.

Fortunately, I owned a textbook on speaking from my college days. At Saint Louis University I was required to take a class on public speaking to complete a business major. The notion of speaking in front of people terrified me. So I postponed taking the class for as long as I could. Finally, second semester senior year, no more slack was in the rope. It was now or never.

The professor came to class impeccably dressed. His hair was so perfect and unchanging that I'm convinced he went to a stylist each day before class. He had a deep, resonant voice that lit up the room when he spoke. He taught that presentations could educate, inspire, engage, motivate, and even transform audiences. He could have sold anything to anyone. But he couldn't sell me on the notion that I'd ever be a public speaker.

On days when I was supposed to present to the class, I'd often pretend to be sick. When I did present, it was from a folded-up paper, as I stared carefully at each word to ensure no eye contact was made with him or the other students. I wasn't sure if I would even pass the class.

On the last day of school the professor asked if he could have a minute of my time. *Uh-oh.*

He walked me back to his office, handed me my final paper, looked me in the eye, and told me, "O'Leary, you got a C in my class. Listen to me: you got a C because I love you. Now, go graduate!"

So in saying yes to that Girl Scout speech, I was in over my head.

More than forty hours went into preparing for that first speech. In the morning I'd tell Beth I had a packed day and would be home late; then I'd tell my employees that I had meetings off-site all day. I'd sit in a vacant parking lot writing, rehearsing, recording, and listening to my speech.

For a week.

For a fifteen-minute talk.

To four third-grade Girl Scouts!

The Wednesday of the presentation, I got up early. Drove out to an abandoned parking lot and practiced for several more hours. I drove by the school around lunchtime to scout out where this thing was going to go down. It's always wise to know the territory of your enemy; to know what you're up against.

I went home. Showered. Put on a suit and tie. Finally, pulled in at three fifteen, opened my door, walked to the front of my car, bent down as if I were going to tie my shoe, and threw up. The immense pressure of speaking to this group literally made me sick.

A little voice whispered to me, *What are you doing? Just go home. This is stupid and so is your story.*

But I got up. I popped in a piece of gum, walked toward the school, and reached for the door. The little voice kept whispering, *They don't really want to hear from you. What if they get bored? What if they throw their coconut-laced Samoas at you? Be smart. Turn around. Quit.*

Inflection point. I had two choices. Shuffle back to my car and claim something came up. Or walk through that door.

I've learned again and again in life that you can show courage or you can be comfortable. But you can't do both at the same time. While comfort might be popular, courage changes lives. I'd seen it with my siblings the day I was burned. Felt it as Nurse Roy carried me down the hallway. Seen it in the eyes of my physical therapists in the hospital. And heard it from Glenn Cunningham when he walked with me.

I ignored the voice, grabbed the door handle, lifted my head, and stepped in.

The girls were all sitting at desks with juice boxes and snacks. The troop leader provided an introduction. I stood behind the teacher's desk, partially read and partially ad-libbed my story. My voice was monotone and shaky. I stumbled over words and lost my place several times. It was far from perfect. When I was done, they asked some questions, applauded sweetly, stood in line, and hugged me before leaving the classroom.

My first speech.

No paycheck for it. No fanfare. No, they didn't even give me a box of cookies.

But that phone call, that one speech, changed the entire

direction of my life. All because I was willing to look up, stretch courageously, and get uncomfortable.

I said yes.

WHAT IF?

I shared my story twice more that year.

A small Catholic school had me speak to their fourth-graders. A local Rotary Club invited me to speak at a luncheon.

As my parents' book continued to circulate, the calls from groups interested in hearing my story expanded, too. I tried to say yes every time. I spoke thirteen times the following year. A few of those events even "paid" me for my time. I got a gas card from one client, a coffee card from another, a tub of popcorn from a third. Baby, I was rolling in it!

Now, no one confused me with Tony Robbins. But with each speech, I got a bit more polished, a little more confident, and a little more convinced this was my intended vocation.

Although the popcorn wasn't going to keep the lights on, after that year, as I saw the impact my story could have on others, I felt compelled to do more than just respond to people who wanted me to speak. I felt a calling to proactively seek opportunities to share my story, to essentially create a speaking business.

I didn't know what I was doing. So I hired a marketing company to help me with a business name, logo, and website.

I bought the website domain name. We incorporated. Made

business cards. And I had all the elements that looked like a real business.

And as you grow a real business, real expenses grow, too. Office space, laptops, software, phone lines, marketing, and, if you are going to grow . . . payroll.

In the early years I was introduced to the perfect candidate to work with me. But there was no way I could afford an employee. She required the exact amount of money that I had made in the previous year. I looked down at my ledger. There just was no way to make it work.

Three days after our initial meeting I got a letter in the mail from her thanking me for the coffee, the time, and the consideration. It ended with a quote from Abraham Lincoln: *Determine that the thing can and shall be done, and then we shall find the way.*

I held the note and read it again.

Okay, I thought. *Well, I'll think about it.*

And I did.

I prayed about it. I asked some friends who ran their own business what they would do. And I discussed the decision with Beth. We examined the possibility of failing, of going into debt, of needing to mortgage the house. We made a list of best-case scenarios and worst-case scenarios. What became clear was the only thing worse than failing in this business might be looking back on not investing and asking, "What if?"

What if I really went All In? What if this could really grow? What if we could inspire others to wake up to the gift of their story? What if this really is my calling?

You see, it doesn't matter if you've finally looked up and seen what is possible, if you are not then willing to choose to stretch, get uncomfortable, and possibly fail to get there.

Vision is worthless without the courage to risk and take action.

You've got to let go in order to reach out. It's like those first few awkward steps I took with the help of my therapist. They'd gently get me on my feet, slowly let go of me, and challenge me to put one foot in front of the other. Each awkward, painful step risking the comforts of where I was for the possibility of a new lease on life.

Was this another moment like that?

Yes.

So I hired Deanna.

This would stretch me into an uncomfortable position unless this thing took off. Trading in my work boots, blue jeans, and tool belt for dress shoes, a suit, and a laptop, I sold all my real estate holdings in 2007 to focus solely on speaking. It was scary. It felt a little crazy. It was an All In play.

And it was the best professional decision of my life.

Our business tripled in the year after I hired Deanna. It's increased every year since. We've moved offices and added amazing colleagues such as Molly, Abby, and additional staff over the years. The little, musty office with one desk has grown into a mission-centered business. Over the past seven years, because of my team's hard work, I've had the honor of speaking to more than half a million people all over the United States and the world. We remain on fire with our mission, our work, and our desire to ignite others to lead inspired lives.

I was twenty-eight years old when I started Rising Above. Life was good. I didn't need to challenge myself to do something that was uncomfortable.

Comfortable is popular, it's easy, it's the currency many trade in.

But boldly stretching is how things grow and where the magic happens. It fuels growth relationally, professionally, and emotionally. It's where lives are changed. Starting with yours.

A VOICE FROM THE PAST

Over four terrible days in April 2011, 355 tornadoes touched down from Texas to New York. Alabama was most directly impacted, with more than 200 tornadoes blasting through the state.

They were the most destructive storms in the history of the state, killing 238 people, causing billions of dollars in damage and devastating entire communities.

As communities slowly began to clean up, the Alabama Power company was challenged with rebuilding its electrical grid. This incredible undertaking would require the entire organization's commitment if it was to be successful.

To encourage their employees to stay safe, to work together, to remain focused on the task at hand, and to remind them that in spite of the terrible storm their best days remained in front of them, I was invited to speak with the various business units.

Speaking more than thirty times all over the state, I fell in love with Alabama Power, with their employees, and with the incredible community they support.

After spending a significant portion of my summer with them, I prepared with mixed emotions my last presentation for the company. The talk was in a beautiful lodge just outside Eufaula, Alabama. I checked in late, got some work done, and went to bed. Nothing special.

The following morning after I finished my final presentation, the man who'd driven me around during the speaking tour and had become a dear friend, Keith, came to the stage. He hugged and thanked me. As I started walking back toward my seat, I heard his southern drawl beckon, "Fella, come on back up here."

Going back to the stage and having no idea what he might do next, I looked at Keith, waiting. He said, "Fella, all summer long you've been shining light into our darkness. We wanted to reflect a little bit of light back your way. So, fella, we wanted to do something kind for you."

Keith had a dozen roses.

He handed them to me.

Wow, thanks, Keith.

Then he said, "Fella, be a good son and give these to your mama."

At the back of the room I saw Mom and Dad appear from behind a curtain. Couldn't believe it. Dad doesn't travel much anymore due to Parkinson's disease. Mom loves any reason to take a vacation, but as Dad's caretaker, she seldom does. As they made their way toward the stage, several hundred power workers rose to their feet.

I hugged my parents, handed the flowers to Mom, and thanked Keith. This was a wonderful surprise.

He went on, "You know, seeing you walk over to your mama and your daddy like that reminded me of that story you told us about the big nurse when you were a little boy. What was his name?"

You mean Nurse Roy?

"Yeah, that was his name. What was it that Roy used to say to you?"

Boy, you're going to walk again. I'll walk with you.

Keith scratched his head and said, "What was is it he used to say?"

I spoke a little louder, *Boy, you are going to walk again. I'll walk with you.*

"No, fella. I bet that he didn't sound like that at all. I bet ya he sounded much more like this."

I heard a microphone kick on. A booming voice filled the room: "Boy, you *are* walking again. And I am proud to walk with you."

I spun around in shock.

They pulled back a curtain in the back of the room and then I saw him. A man I hadn't seen in twenty-four years. Nurse freaking Roy!

He hadn't aged. He still looked just like Apollo Creed.

I started to walk down the aisle toward him. The audience leaped to their feet again and applause rained down.

I had kept in touch with many of the nurses and doctors who had served me all those years ago. An entire table at my wedding reception was filled with those friends. But Roy had left the hospital shortly after my release; we'd never been able to find him. Alabama Power had tracked down this amazing man who was so instrumental to my story. They contacted him, explained to him how I spoke about him, and asked if they could fly him in to reunite with me.

Apparently he'd said yes because now he was giving me a huge bear hug.

I was speechless.

Tears filled my eyes.

What a moment.

Mom, Dad, Roy, and I sat down to dinner that night. The last time we'd eaten together, I was on morphine, tied to a bed, with nutrition coming in through a feeding tube. Now we were sitting at dinner, flanked by new friends from Alabama Power, celebrating this amazing reunion, and absolutely on fire with joy. It was a night I'll never forget.

Near the end of the night Roy and I had a few minutes by ourselves to reconnect. We talked about my time in the hospital, those brutal bandage changes, and the daily walks to the tub. We talked about difficult nurses and old friends. We shared what we'd both been up to for the last twenty-four years. I told him about my family; he shared with me about his. He then leaned over and said, "You know, John, it surprises me that you did something with your life."

The same sentiment has been shared with me several times by high school teachers from my past. But this time I felt it was intended as a compliment. You see, when a child is burned, sometimes he or she makes it out of the hospital, but not back into life. The emotional journey is just too painful. I understood what Roy was saying.

So I said, "Thanks, Roy."

"You know what surprises me even more, though?"

I shook my head no.

"How you were able to marry such a beautiful woman!" He chuckled.

"Wow. Thanks, Roy. I am glad they found you!"

We both laughed.

Then he said, "John, in all seriousness, do you know what surprises me the most about all of this? About this dinner, this reunion, this whole thing?"

"I don't think I want to hear this one, Roy!"

"Well, I am going to tell you."

He took a sip of his ice water. He looked into my eyes. He took a long pause. Then he said, "It is to learn that after twenty-four years, I mattered. John, I did my job, I loved my work, I loved my patients. But I never really understood until today that I mattered."

"You did, man. You did." I swallowed, the emotion catching

up with me. But this was my moment to tell Roy what he really did for that little boy.

"Roy, I loved all my nurses. They were all so good to me. But truth be told, some of them would be whispering to each other about death. They didn't really believe. You, Roy, would walk into that same room, to that same burned-up little boy, pick me up, and basically yell at me, 'Forget death! Boy, you are going to walk!' Roy, you changed my life. Yeah, you mattered. I'll never forget you."

What an awesome reminder not just for a kid in a burn center, but for each of us as we stretch forward in our work, health, faith, relationships, and lives. Forget death. You are going to live. You are going to walk. And I'll walk with you.

Lift your head.

Walk on.

STAGNATION V. GROWTH

*The most pathetic person in the world is someone who has sight,
but has no vision.*
—Helen Keller

What's really possible through your life?

This is a question that can't be fully answered if you're looking down at
your feet.

This is your inflection point.

Anxiety and fear will keep you stagnant. *What if I fail? What if I am too
old? What if I never walk again?* In looking down, all you see is your
shoes, the dirt; all you feel is discouragement, struggle.

But you can choose instead to look up, stretch, and breathe life and
possibility into every moment.

This is your day. Put your cape back on. Remember the powerful
possibility that lived in your heart as a child. Begin daring to dream
again.

*What if this is just the beginning? What if I actually could succeed? What if
I can make a profound impact in another's life? What if I stretched actively
forward each day?*

Isn't it time to risk it all in order to build something, inspire another, and
become someone great?

Isn't it time to stretch courageously toward the limitless possibility of
your life?

Isn't it time you get moving, start dreaming, and begin growing?

Growth is the only evidence of life.

Choose growth.

Do your little bit of good where you are;
it's those little bits of good put together that
overwhelm the world.

—DESMOND TUTU

6

WHAT MORE CAN YOU DO?

One life can, and always does, change the world.

*I*t happened yesterday.

I was just lying in my hospital bed.

I couldn't move. (I'm strapped to the bed.)

I couldn't talk. (The ventilator prevents it.)

I couldn't see. (My eyes are swollen shut.)

I was in the dark, in pain and totally scared.

But also dreaming, hoping, and praying.

And listening.

Intently.

I hear everything going on around me. I can't do much else, so that's what I do. Listen.

It was in listening that I was blown away.

You see, I like sports. All sports. But I love baseball. The St. Louis Cardinals are my team. I love watching the games, but we don't go to the stadium very often.

And the games are only on the TV a few times a year.

So the way we watch baseball in our house isn't with our eyes. Nope. It's with our ears.

We listen to the radio.

We listen to announcers.

We listen to a guy named Jack Buck. He's the voice of the St. Louis Cardinals. He's the guy I listen to all summer long. Who tells me what my Cardinals are doing. He's the one I listen to in my bedroom under the blankets long after I am supposed to be asleep. And even though I've never met him, I love him!

And he's also the guy who walked into my room yesterday.

That's right. Jack Buck visited me in my hospital room.

I couldn't see him.

But I didn't need to.

I was just lying in bed listening to the beeping of the machines that were keeping me alive when I heard the door open.

I heard footsteps.

I heard a chair get dragged across the floor.

I heard a cough.

And then I heard a voice.

"Kid. Wake up."

I recognized his voice right away.

It was Jack Buck.

"Listen to me. You are going to live. You got that? You are going

to survive. And when you get out of here, we are going to celebrate! We'll call it John O'Leary Day at the ballpark."

Jack Buck. In my room? Talking to me? I couldn't believe it!

"Kid, are you listening to me?"

I couldn't move anything, but tried to nod my head as much as I could. I wanted him to know that I was listening.

He must have noticed because he said, "Good."

He didn't say anything for a long time. I figured he left.

Then I heard him say, "Keep fighting, kid."

I heard the chair get pushed back, footsteps walk away from me, the door slide open, and Jack Buck left the room.

It was a short visit.

When he left, I was still tied down to the bed, eyes swollen shut, unable to move, unable to speak, unable to do anything.

But I was absolutely, totally fired up!

Yeah, man, we were going to have a party! "John O'Leary Day at the ballpark!" I like the sound of that!

That was yesterday. And I've been thinking about those words, that promise, and that voice ever since. In fact, it's all I can think about today. Yes, I'm still in pain. Yes, there's still beeping. Yes, there's still the Darth Vader breathing noise from the respirator. But I'm not focused on that anymore. I'm thinking about that visit and my day at the ballpark.

Then I hear my door open up.

Footsteps of someone walking in.

A chair gets pulled across the floor.

There's a cough.

Then I hear a voice.

"Kid. Wake up. I'm back!"

Oh my gosh! It's him again.

"Kid, listen to me. You are going to live, got that? You are going to survive. And when you get out of here, we are going to celebrate. We will call it John O'Leary Day at the ballpark. Kid, keep fighting."

There's a long pause.

Then I hear, "See you soon."

The chair gets pushed back across the floor.

The door opens up.

I'm alone again. The room is filled with the sound of beeping.

Beep. Beep. Beep.

I'm still in darkness.

Tied to the bed.

Can't move.

Can't see.

Can't talk.

By myself.

With a single thought: wait until my friends hear about this!

Jack Buck changed my life.

He entered into it just a few days after I was burned.

The odds of surviving remained overwhelmingly slight. Because of the high likelihood of infection, the only individuals allowed into my room were essential staff members and my parents. At the time there was a strict rule: absolutely no visitors.

That changed when Jack Buck walked into the burn center looking for a little boy who had been burned the previous weekend. The staff consulted with my parents and reminded them that a visitor in my room might introduce an infection. But a visit from a Hall of Fame announcer that their little boy idolized, hanging on each word during the baseball season, would also unquestionably introduce hope. The choice was made to allow him in.

He'd never met me or my family. He'd simply been told that a little boy in the community had been injured, faced terrible odds, and needed some encouragement. That was enough for Jack.

He scrubbed up, gowned up, walked into my room and into my life.

He was unprepared for the beeping, the warning lights, the respirator's loud gurgling noises, the little boy stretched out on a bed wrapped literally head to toe with bandages. I later learned his first visit was so short because he became so emotional he could no longer speak. After telling me to keep fighting, he left the room, ripped off the scrubs and broke down weeping in the hallway.

A nurse came over to comfort him. After all, they didn't get celebrities in the burn center every day. And they certainly couldn't have the biggest celebrity in St. Louis break down on the floor!

She asked if he was okay.

Jack replied he wasn't sure. He asked if the little boy was going to make it.

The nurse shook her head no and explained the extent of my injuries. She then shared, "Mr. Buck, I am sorry, there just isn't a chance. It's just his time."

He left the burn center with this information.

Jack had done his good deed. He had visited a dying kid in the hospital. He owed me nothing.

He had done enough.

He had learned that some climbs are just too steep; this little boy would not survive this one. There was not a chance.

Not a chance.

And in spite of all the reasons to give up hope and move on with his life, the following day Jack came back.

An unlikely friendship would play out during my stay in the hospital. Jack made frequent visits; talked about me on broadcasts; and sent professional baseball, football, and hockey players to my room once visitors were allowed. Jack did everything in his power to encourage me to keep battling, to fight for John O'Leary Day at the ballpark.

In my scariest, bleakest days, one man's voice shone light into my darkness. One visit gave me a promise to cling to. One voice echoed hope.

And he only got the chance to have such an impact because one person told him my story.

STARTING THE FIRE

Fire is the most destructive element in nature.

Sweeping waves of flame consume everything in their path. Everything is scorched; nothing is spared.

Take the Buckweed Fire, which started in a rural community in the northern part of Los Angeles County in 2007. Fanned by high winds and dry weather, it spread quickly. This single fire forced fifteen thousand people from their homes, destroyed dozens of structures, and charred more than thirty-eight thousand acres. And it all started with a little boy, playing with a single match. This can be the impact of one person, making one poor decision.

Ah, but a single spark can also be harnessed for good.

Fire, a source for heat, cooks our food, warms our houses, and toasts our marshmallows. It strengthens steel, forms glass, powers engines. And in nature, despite its initial destruction, it is necessary for forests to thrive.

You see, fire clears out deadwood, removes old vegetation, fertilizes the land with life-giving nutrients, breaks open seeds, and triggers new growth. Some seeds require fire to soften their outer shell after the seed falls to the earth, so it can take root and grow. Just a year after devastating forest fires new life is already flourishing. Within a decade the forest is once again vibrant.

Such is the power of a single spark to leap, to be harnessed, to ignite others, and to trigger a righteous inferno.

The day I was burned, the news of our fire and the seemingly insurmountable odds against a little boy's survival spread quickly. Years before social media, this tragedy went viral in our community. Neighbors, friends, and family members were the first to learn. They'd then share with others, encouraging prayers and action for this family that had lost a house and was likely to lose a child.

In one life-changing example, my next-door neighbor called a friend, who told another friend, who shared the news with her neighbor Colleen Schoendienst. Stoking the fire, she then called her dad and asked if he would keep a little boy from our community in his prayers.

That phone call changed my life.

Colleen's father, baseball great Red Schoendienst, went to a charity event that night. He sat next to his friend Jack Buck and mentioned that a little boy was not expected to live after being burned earlier in the day.

That was the extent of the conversation.

But it was enough.

The impact of a simple spark is profound. Sometimes the smallest actions, words, and deeds transform lives. Certainly the short visits and encouragement from Jack Buck changed mine.

But it really wasn't just Jack, was it?

It was Red.

Without his sharing the news, Jack would never have known, never visited, never inspired me. So the credit goes to Red.

Well, actually, it wasn't Red, either.

It was Colleen.

She made the phone call; she told her father about the fire. She's the reason Red knew. She's the reason Jack found out. She's the reason I'm alive.

Right?

Or was it her neighbor?

Or the friend?

Or my next-door neighbor?

My friend, we frequently cheapen our ability to influence radical change. We underestimate our personal ability to be a spark that ignites and influences the world in profoundly important ways.

We possess the ability and opportunity to positively and permanently effect change around us.

Simple action and ordinary people change the world.

It starts with one.

It starts with you.

But you have to pay attention.

A SIMPLE QUESTION

It should have been a quick answer.

I'd just finished speaking in a conference room full of educators. As I met the teachers afterward and signed books, a woman in her midforties approached, introduced herself, and gave me a hug. She handed me a book to sign. I wrote her name, a note of encouragement, signed it, and handed the book back to her.

She looked at me, down at my hands, and asked, "How'd you learn to do it? How'd you learn to write?"

Do you have a minute?

She nodded and I shared with her how I'd learned to write despite my lack of fingers.

A month after I came home from the hospital we packed up the station wagon. Mom and Dad got in the front; six kids clad in red squeezed behind them. It was early evening and hot; our backs stuck to the red vinyl seats as we headed downtown. This was the day we'd been looking forward to since the first time Jack Buck had come into my room. It was John O'Leary Day at the ballpark. This was going to rock!

Jack met us at the press entrance and personally pushed my wheelchair into the stadium. He chauffeured me into the depths of the stadium, through a narrow hallway, past a few ushers and players. Making a left-hand turn, the dark, narrow tunnel opened into the dugout. Up three steps was a vista of bright green Astro-Turf, red seats, and a baseball diamond. Dad and Jack carried my wheelchair up the steps and onto the field.

The opposing team took batting practice. I gawked at the size of the stadium from the field.

Jack then rolled me off the field, back into the darkened tunnel, past an assembly of police officers and ushers, and into a room marked ST. LOUIS CARDINALS CLUBHOUSE. He pushed me in, rolled me around the room, and one by one introduced me to each player by name. The only thing more stunning than meeting my boyhood idols was meeting them while they were completely naked! It was like a freaking Greek bathhouse! They were all in various stages of undress, completely comfortable with it, and incredibly kind to this little boy rolled into their space before the game.

It was an experience I'll never forget.

We then took an elevator to the luxury-box level. This was certainly an unbelievable treat for our family.

Mom and my siblings were escorted to a box overlooking third base.

Jack shepherded Dad and me to his office, the broadcaster's box positioned directly behind home plate. It had a perfect, panoramic view of the stadium. The box was tiered with two seating areas, one in the first row and the other five steps behind. That night, in the first row, sat the radio producer, an announcer named Mike Shannon, another named Jack Buck, and a nine-year-old, wheelchair-bound little boy with bright red skin, splints on his arms, legs, and neck, bandages covering much of his body, a Cardinals hat on his head, and a big, massive smile plastered on his face.

John O'Leary Day at the ballpark was everything I dreamed it would be.

After almost four hours of baseball, the Cardinals won the game in extra innings on a home run. I went home with eight empty plastic cups that had previously held soda. I went home with souvenirs: baseballs, jerseys, and bats. And I went home with a tape of the broadcast that recorded Jack repeatedly spoon-feeding me beautiful questions and me responding with remarkably forgettable one-word answers to every question.

"Well, it's been a day we've all been looking forward to. After a long battle in the hospital my little friend is well enough to be with us tonight. It's John O'Leary Day at the ballpark, and this brave boy is sitting next to me. Kid, are you having fun?"

In a high-pitched, nervous voice I spoke into an oversize microphone.

Yes.

"You were in a fire in January. Spent months in the hospital and endured dozens of surgeries. I bet you are glad to be out of there and back at home."

Yes.

"I understand you love baseball. The Cardinals are your team. You think this team can win us a World Series this year?"

Yes.

And so the interview went. Riveting radio.

But you know what? Jack didn't focus on my answers. He was too busy paying attention to something much more important.

He saw a little kid unable to get out of a wheelchair, unable to use his arms or body, unable to use his hands. Jack realized as the night progressed that this little kid had survived, he was back home, he was celebrating at the ballpark.

But the real fight was just beginning.

And he chose to encourage me to keep fighting.

A few days later I received a package in the mail. My mom

helped me unwrap it, and there, nestled in paper, was a baseball autographed by our All-Star shortstop, Ozzie Smith. Beneath the ball was a note from Jack.

Kid, if you want a second baseball, you'll have to write a thank you note to the man who signed the first. Your friend, Jack Buck

Write a thank-you note?

Um, was he kidding?

I could barely hold anything, let alone a pen. Hadn't he been watching as my dad held my cup so I could drink those eight sodas?

Of course he'd noticed that.

Jack Buck paid attention.

And that's why he'd sent the baseball.

Mom and Dad had been pleading with me to try to write again. The therapists were working with me to write again. They kept reminding me that the sooner I learned to write the sooner I could go back to school.

Was that supposed to be motivational? I didn't like school!

But I loved baseball.

I sure wanted another autographed ball.

Here was another example of when you know your *why*, you can endure any *how*.

With my hands still wrapped in bandages, I asked Mom to help me hold a pen to paper and write a thank-you note. It was painful, took several attempts, and was barely legible. But it thanked Ozzie for the ball, was mailed to him, and included my name.

Without my even knowing it, this was a mighty inflection point in my journey. The first step toward writing, toward school, toward *normalcy*, was taken that day. And at the time I thought it was just about getting a second baseball.

Three days later, I received a second baseball in the mail, with a second note.

Kid, if you want a third baseball, all you have to do is write a thank you note. Your friend, Jack Buck

"Mom! Come in here. Quick. And bring a pen!"

Another thank-you note went out.

A few days later another baseball arrived.

Kid, if you want a fourth baseball . . .

Are you beginning to see the pattern here?!

By the time the St. Louis Cardinals played in the World Series that October, a little boy in St. Louis had received sixty baseballs and sent sixty thank-you notes.

Several months after John O'Leary Day at the ballpark, some burned-up "kid" with no fingers and no chance was back in school.

All because one man paid attention.

And then he asked one simple but essential question: *What more can I do?*

In asking this question he saw possibility where others saw limitations, took action where others watched idly, and focused on making a difference for others.

This simple question demanded action when he sat at a charity auction and learned that a little boy was burned. *What more can I do? Okay . . . I'll visit him.*

This simple question provided persistence after that original visit when the staff told him that the little boy was going to die. *They think it's hopeless. Well, what more can I do? Okay . . . I'll visit him again so that he can believe it's possible.*

This question guided him to visit me throughout my time in the hospital, to keep the promise of John O'Leary Day at the ballpark, and to send sixty baseballs afterward. *What more can I do?*

This man had a thriving career, a busy family life, probably his own struggles, but he took the time to ask what more he could do for that little boy. I'm forever grateful.

What are you paying attention to? Most of us pay attention to our own problems. We look at our to-do list, our balance sheet, our waistline, our kids. We spend our days looking at our phones, checking our e-mail, scrolling through our Facebook posts.

But what did Jack do?

He looked at others.

He paid attention to what was going on around him.

Not for what he could get out of the situation. But for what he could give.

This is the difference between a life of success and a life of significance.

It's the difference between a quick win and a true victory.

TRUE VICTORY

I introduced you to Glenn Cunningham already.

You know, the man who was terribly burned as a kid, learned to walk, started running, became an Olympian, and decades later encouraged me to never quit?

Well, if you read the *Wikipedia* article about him, that's all you'd know because it describes his burns as a boy and recovery afterward. It describes his rise through the ranks of running—beginning in high school, then college, on to the Olympics, and culminating in Glenn's being regarded as the number one runner in the world. It lists races, locations, times, and finishes. It mentions he retired in 1940. But I would argue that the forty-eight years between his retirement and his death were the most magnificent and impressive aspect of his life—and perhaps any life.

You see, after coming home from the Olympics, Glenn got married and began to raise a family on a large ranch in Kansas. He and his wife, Ruth, had three children when they learned about a Russian family who had been displaced during World War II. Glenn and Ruth discussed this family, their needs, and eventually invited this struggling family to live in their tenant house for a few years.

After he retired from running, Glenn began speaking to groups around the country. He was so inspiring, faithful, and clearly of high character that letters began arriving at his ranch from audience members. They'd thank him for his time, his story, his accomplishments, and his encouragement. One note even told the story of a struggling child, the challenges he faced, and ended with the parent of the struggling young boy asking, *Could Tommy come stay at your ranch for a bit?*

Glenn and Ruth already had three kids. They were busy on the ranch and life was hectic on the road.

But they also felt a slight tug of discontent, believing that they could do more. After all, they had plenty of land, owned a twelve-room house, and weren't filling it up. With some creativity and frugalness, they decided they could financially support another child for a while. What would it hurt to have one more kid to fill those rooms and join the family?

So they said yes.

Glenn and Ruth proved to be outstanding parents and guardians. Soon, other families were writing asking if their kid could stay at the ranch. The Cunninghams' answer was always the same: yes.

The courts soon started sending troubled youth. Before they knew it, the Cunninghams' home was overflowing with kids of all ages. Some stayed for a few days or for a few weeks. Some stayed for the summer. A few stayed for years.

Eventually, Glenn and Ruth had twelve children of their own. But they made no distinction between those they brought in from the outside and those born of their own flesh and blood. The children were all considered the Cunninghams' own and received unconditional love. In return these kids were expected to follow rules, do chores, and help take care of the animals on the ranch. In other words, they were part of the family.

Ruth and Glenn opened wide their hearts and their home. Over more than four decades they had served, raised, fostered, and encouraged more than nine thousand children.

Nine freaking thousand kids!

Not many people today can say that.

It wasn't easy financially. It was endless work for both of them. But they made room for those children, knowing whatever love and respect they could provide to them would make a difference in their lives.

Glenn clearly knew the power of the question *What more can I do?*

It guided him from a hospital bed with severe burns on his legs to a podium with medals around his neck. It motivated him from his comfortable house with three kids to his being a change agent for good, impacting thousands of youth. And it elevated him from a life of success and status to one of significance and impact.

The world celebrates status. The Olympic medal. The big house. The beautiful face. The victory. But the metals deteriorate. The house ages. The beautiful face sags. The victories we clamor for often end up feeling hollow.

The individuals who attain the highest forms of achievement

in life don't sprint toward success, but significance. They don't run races, build businesses, raise kids, and live lives for themselves; they do these things to make a difference for others. They hold hands, move hearts, give love, and impact lives. Through these actions, achieving this kind of victory, the fire burns long after they are gone.

Glenn Cunningham made an incredible life, not by what he did, but by what he gave.

You don't need to be an Olympian to start.

You just need to serve where you're able.

You just need to live a yes life.

LIVING YES

I worked for three years as a hospital chaplain.

It was part-time work primarily on nights and weekends. The first year I served adults. The next couple of years, some of the most transformative of my life, were spent with children and their families at a pediatric hospital.

In these visits with injured, sick, or dying little ones, it became clear what matters. For these families, the former concerns of perfect grades, athleticism, the right sport teams, and popularity faded. The stress and race of a jam-packed schedule to elevate a child in as many areas as possible, preparing them for a life of success, was wiped clear. Time was instead spent anticipating test results, praying in waiting rooms, dreaming of a future, any future, and relishing face-to-face conversations. These scared parents and their amazing little ones fought forward together for health, normalcy, and life.

They were fully awake to what actually mattered.

Many times I'd leave these interactions, walk out to my car, close the door, and just weep. I'd be brokenhearted by the mighty challenges in front of them, but also radically inspired by their zest for life and love of one another.

One experience and one family in particular remain with me today.

While visiting with a little girl who shared my great passion for baseball and love of vanilla ice cream, my pager vibrated. I looked down at it and saw a room number followed by 4444. My stomach turned.

This is the code we used when a patient's heart had stopped; a child was no longer breathing. It beckoned a medical team to race toward the room. Together they'd work to revive the little one.

Chaplains are part of this team to emotionally support the staff and pray for the kids, and if the parents are there, to sit with them through the terror.

In TV shows such as *ER* or *Grey's Anatomy*, when a code occurs a couple of good-looking doctors race toward a room. Sarah McLachlan music plays dramatically in the background. The doctors typically inject a few drugs, push a few buttons, and life magically returns. The song finishes, the doctors hug, and we cut to commercial.

In real life there is no music, it's a brutal process, and life seldom returns.

This was all on my mind as I raced from my seven-year-old friend, down a hallway, into the ICU, and toward the room. I saw the mother and father of this little patient standing outside the room. Watching. Observing something terrible that no parent should ever have to see.

I walked over to them, introduced myself, explained what was happening, and offered to walk them to a private waiting room. I didn't want them to have to see this. I didn't want the potential last memories of their child to be these moments.

The young mother turned to me, looked me sternly in the eyes, and said, "John, we're not going anywhere. Whether you like it or not, we are with our baby. Life . . . or death."

She turned away from me, leaned into her husband, and looked back toward her child.

We stood outside the room and watched. We watched doctors taking turns climbing on top of the bed to do forceful compressions on the child's chest. We watched repeated injections of various medicines administered by staff. We watched nurses taking turns squeezing oxygen into his little lungs. Eventually, we watched as a young doctor, noticeably crushed by the loss, approached and explained that they could do nothing more: "Your child is now with God."

The mother pushed past the physician, through the gathered staff, and to her two-year-old son. She bent down over the bed, brushed back his hair, picked him up, and held him in her arms. She gently swayed with him and lightly sang to him.

The rest of the staff walked out of the room.

The father and I walked in.

We didn't say a word.

We just stood together in this sacred, tragic, surreal moment.

I've discovered that saying nothing during times of great emotion is often the best form of communication. A young couple can stroll a park, hand in hand, and not once say anything. A parent can sit with a child, watching waves roll in, the sun go down, birds fly past, and not say a thing. Two dear friends can sit rocking on a front porch without feeling the need to fill the time with idle words.

During tragedy, the same is true. When we get diagnosed with a difficult disease, when we lose a dear friend, when things fall apart in our lives, we seldom long for someone to come in and fix it with words. No words will ever take away our pain. No, we long for someone to have the courage to be with us, sit there with us, cry with us. In other words, we want someone to be fully present with us.

So we just stood, together, quietly.

Eventually, the father put his arm around me and said, "John, do you know that this little guy was the one? We have three children, nine, seven, and this little one. But this was the one. He was the one who made our family complete. He was just two, but he taught us what life is about. He lit up each day for us and made them brighter than any day before it."

He continued, "You probably don't know this, but he was born sick. He was never supposed to leave the hospital, but we got to take him home. We got to love him. We had him for two years. Two incredible years."

The man's wife continued rocking their child, and he continued sharing details of the child's life. I stood next to the man, his arm around me, tears pouring down my cheeks.

"Now, things weren't easy. He never learned to sit up, never learned to speak, never learned to communicate, but like I said, he was the one."

An intense quiet again filled the room.

The mother continued rocking her child.

She then looked up from the little boy and said to her husband, "Tell him about the notes that we got from the principal earlier this week."

Monday afternoon a note had come home from the principal at the school where their two older boys attended. It thanked them for raising such incredible young men. The note explained what a joy it was to have these two students in the school and then provided two vivid examples: "Your boys are the only boys in the entire school who push kids in wheelchairs class to class. They do it without being asked and without looking for acknowledgment. And your boys are the only boys in school who sit at lunchtime with kids who have special needs. There is a large room of happy, rambunctious kids eating and only one table of kids who have some challenges. Your boys are always sitting there with them."

The father finished speaking, and I was overwhelmed with emotion.

As a child, I had had some special needs.

As a man, I'm married to a woman who works with kids with special needs.

Hearing this heartbroken father proudly proclaim this story, while watching his wife rock their lifeless son, touched me profoundly.

I asked the dad, *Is it because of this little boy, this little miracle, that your other two kids are the way they are?*

The mother responded, "John, because of him, I am a better mom, he's a better dad, my boys are better boys, and we will all, always, be better."

I'm a better mom.

He's a better dad.

My boys are better boys.

And we'll all, always, be better.

I'll never forget this experience, that conversation, those parents, that perfect little boy. That little boy taught his brothers to pay attention. Their little brother helped open their eyes to the question "What more can I do?" He was the spark that set fire to that family's life. Would they miss their little boy, their brother, every day of their lives?

Absolutely.

But they lived each day in an inspired way because he had come into their lives.

Was his life a success?

Many would say no.

But was his life significant?

Did he make a difference?

Did he positively impact others?

Profoundly.

THE POWER OF ONE

I have a simple rule: don't argue with nuns.

I learned this rule gradually from the many nuns I've come across through grade school, while I was sick in the hospital, and in my years as a chaplain.

A simple nun once wrote, "I alone cannot change the world. But I can cast a stone across the water to create many ripples."

This quote comes from an impoverished, frail Albanian lady who took a train to one of the poorest countries in the world, sought out the poorest city, ventured into the poorest alleys, and began quietly serving those she found there. One by one she fed, held, humanized, and loved the people she served. She attracted others to her cause. A movement began. Now, the order she founded, the Missionaries of Charity, claims forty-five hundred religious sisters serving in more than 130 countries around the world. Even though their leader is gone, the order she began continues to care for refugees, children, lepers, people with AIDS, the aged, and the dying. They are a mighty agent for good in a world starved for it.

Because of one woman.

Volumes have been written on Mother Teresa. Books share her childhood, conversion, challenges, passion, love, faith, and even how she wrestled with doubt much of her life.

But let there be no doubt about this: her life is an example of the truth that one life can and always does change the world.

We need not travel to India to find examples.

We all have examples in our own lives. If we look for them.

After I finish presenting, individuals often approach and share their personal stories. They share stories of how their lives were improved because men and women, ordinary people, supported, offered encouragement, and took action.

One week I was invited to speak three different times, by three different organizations, over three consecutive days. The locations were in New York, Missouri, and Illinois. After each, people lined up to share their stories and the individuals who had positively impacted them along their journey.

In New York, a man told a story of being at JFK Airport years ago, ordering his lunch, and preparing to pay for it. And then he heard a deep, gravelly voice from just behind him in line, "I'll get his lunch." He turned around to see a man he thought he recognized. The stranger introduced himself as Jack Buck. Before the man could even speak, Jack handed payment to the cashier. The man shared that he was a die-hard Mets fan, but that day he stopped hating the Cardinals and started loving Jack Buck.

It was awesome hearing another example of how Jack Buck lit up someone's day. Even if the guy was a Mets fan.

The following day in Missouri, a man came up and talked about his years as a starving artist. He was struggling so mightily that he took a job painting houses. He made just over minimum wage.

On a hot summer day, while he was painting second-floor windows on a house, a raspy voice called him down from the ladder and insisted he take a break. The man who owned the house invited the painter to take his break inside and cool off. While drinking lemonade at Jack Buck's kitchen table, Russell Irwin shared that he loved painting, but preferred canvas to window sashes. He shared his frustration and his inability to showcase his talent to the world.

Jack listened, asked questions, paid attention, and came up with a plan. Jack invited the artist to create a painting of all of the St. Louis Cardinals Hall of Famers. They made 250 copies and sold them for charity. The efforts raised more than $500,000. It also launched Russell Irwin's career.

I couldn't believe it. Another story of Jack Buck and the way he could change people's lives in the simplest ways.

Finally, the following day after I spoke in Illinois, a man approached me. He talked about his first time speaking to a group of his peers. He was to speak in front of four hundred colleagues, to give opening remarks at a sales meeting. Prepared with notes, he marched up to the podium, looked at the crowd, back to his notes, and completely froze.

The man was simply unable to speak.

There was a long, awkward silence.

A mumble of scattered laughing came from around the room.

Then a white-haired man walked up from the audience. He came over to the podium. He put his arm around the speaker. He read the first line from the notes, then said, "Okay, kid, I think you can take it from here."

That's right. It was Jack Buck.

The stage-frightened gentleman delivered his remarks. He told me it was a turning point in his career and life. He is now the COO of the organization and has emceed the gala for each of the past thirteen years. He credits his success to an inflection point early in his career, when words wouldn't come, when everyone else remained silent, and when Jack Buck stepped forward.

One person.

Taking simple actions.

Changing the lives of others.

Jack was extremely successful professionally.

He was a Hall of Fame announcer, beloved in his community both for his voice and his charm. For decades he was the top play-by-play announcer in all of sports.

Yet, after getting to know the man, meeting his kids, speaking with his wife, and hearing stories of his impact from others all around the country, I am convinced I know the secret to his success: his life wasn't about him.

It was just that simple. He didn't keep score. His work wasn't about his earning power. His time wasn't about what he could get. Renowned as a celebrity, he had no ego.

He paid attention to others around him—and took action to

make their lives better. His actions weren't loud, weren't overly heroic, weren't that costly. But by his consistent investment in others the ripple effect of his life radiates outward long after his death.

Jack certainly chose to lead a radically inspired life. **He's the perfect example of the sixth choice in action: the key to true greatness in life is to choose to pursue significance over success.**

He sought significance.

And in doing so attracted success.

So can one person make a difference?

The answer is an absolute, reverberating, and joyful *Yes!* But the power of one requires belief.

You must believe.

By now you are familiar with my story.

The fire.

The burns.

The slim chances.

The miracle.

Either I am the luckiest guy in the world, or something is going on here.

The truth is, every step of the way, some individuals were delivering the facts: a burn on 100 percent of your body means no chance of surviving. The little boy isn't going to make it. It's his time. There just is no chance. Okay. So he lived, but what kind of life will it really be? He certainly won't walk, he'll never write, he'll not actively contribute, he'll never return to "normal."

Fortunately, at every step of the way, others believed, fought, and prayed.

Jim. Swinging into the flames, risking his life for mine.

Amy. Holding on to me and assuring me the best is yet to come.

Susan. Running into a burning house for water.

Mom. Grasping my hand and reminding me to take the hand of God.

Roy. Carrying me upright and reminding me, *Boy, forget death. You are going to walk.*

Jack. *Kid! Wake up! You are going to live!*

These people believed. They had faith. They knew it could get better. This didn't have to be the end.

Believing in the power of one allows us to see where we could make a difference. It allows us to see the opportunity of *What more can I do?* It jars us from sleepiness, wakes us up to pay attention, and demands that we take action.

In my experience, believing that God works through all things frees me from the stress of worrying each day, being weighed down by the tragedies around me, and ignites me with certainty that the best is yet to come. I believe that God is all-knowing, all-loving, and all-powerful. And I believe that because God frequently works through our words, deeds, and love, we must remain open to his will in our lives.

Believing opens your heart to love, your eyes to possibility, and your life to the truth that your life, that every life, matters profoundly.

PRICELESS

I graduated college.

You've read this far into this book and you still don't believe miracles can happen? Well, there is proof right there! Somehow, this high-spirited but academically unmotivated kid graduated college.

Another miracle appeared the night of graduation.

I never dated in grade school. Never dated in high school. And the drought continued during four years of college. But graduation night it rained, the miracle of love appeared.

Consider for a moment what she might look like?

No, don't cheat and look at the picture in the back!

Just shut your eyes and for a moment consider what love looked like.

You got her in mind?

No, think again. Not that kind of love.

The love that appeared graduation night wasn't physical, it wasn't sexual, it wasn't the beginning of a lifelong partnership. Instead it was the incredible generosity of Jack Buck flowing once more into my life.

We'd kept up our friendship over the years.

In learning that the boy who didn't have a chance to survive the fire, and certainly had no chance to write again, was now graduating college, Jack dropped off a gift for me.

At a dinner celebrating my graduation, surrounded by family, I was handed a beautifully wrapped box with a short note from Jack Buck.

The first word read, "Kid." (At times I wonder if Jack ever knew my name!)

The note went on, "This means a lot to me. I hope it means a lot to you, too."

I unwrapped the present, opened the box, looked inside, and saw another baseball. But this one was different. It was heavy. It appeared dark. It seemed to be made out of glass. Stepping away from the table and the darkened dining room, I walked outside, seeking light to see what it was.

I opened the door of the restaurant and, as the sun set, pulled the ball out of the box and held it into the light. Glinting off the crystal baseball I saw the engraving "Jack Buck. Baseball Hall of Fame. 1987."

That was the year I was burned.

It was also the year Jack was inducted into the Baseball Hall of Fame.

This was Jack Buck's Hall of Fame baseball.

I lost my breath and looked back at his note.

Kid, this means a lot to me. I hope it means a lot to you, too. This is the baseball I received when I was inducted into the Hall of Fame. It's made of crystal. It's priceless. Don't drop it! Your friend, Jack

I looked again at this priceless gift.

Why would Jack Buck give me such a treasured possession?

With the ball glimmering before me, I felt woefully undeserving of this gift. This baseball should have been on display in his home. This should have been passed on to the next generation in his family. This should not have been mine.

I was a twenty-two-year-old kid. I was scared of my own shadow. I had no idea who I was or what life was all about. I was so overwhelmed by the gift that I took it home that night and buried it in my sock drawer.

I didn't want anyone to see this gift that I felt unworthy of receiving. I knew if someone saw it, they might ask how I got it. Then I might have to tell them how I came to know Jack. Then I might have to share my scars, my story. I wasn't prepared for that.

So I kept it to myself.

I hid it.

In darkness.

For years.

But light always overcomes darkness. Sometimes it just takes time to chase the shadows.

When Jack gave me the ball, he had no idea that someday my dad would be stricken with the same ailment Jack battled, Parkinson's disease. He had no idea my parents would write a book. He had no idea one day the kid would grow up, embrace his scars, and share his story. Jack had no idea that hundreds of thousands of people around the world would be inspired by his gift, his generosity, the way he stepped into my life. He likely had no idea just how bright the light might shine.

Jack gave for a much simpler reason.

He gave because he could.

In doing so he radically inspired my life.

I think of Jack all the time. I think of his voice bringing light into my darkness in the hospital. I think of John O'Leary Day at the ballpark. I think of those sixty baseballs arriving in the mail, teaching me to write again. Every time I see his crystal baseball shimmering, reflecting light around the room, I think of how one person can make a difference.

I also think of him every time I'm with my oldest son. Jack Buck would love my ten-year-old son. He'd love his name, too.

Jack.

SUCCESS V. SIGNIFICANCE

*We make a living by what we get; we make a life
by what we give.*
—Winston Churchill

We're all busy.

We all have innumerable responsibilities, tasks, and chores. You may be feeling, *Gosh, I can't do one more thing. I am maxed out with my family, my job, the bills. What more can I do?*

Here is your inflection point. Instead of throwing up your hands and saying, "Gosh, what *more* can I do?"—open up your heart, reach out your hand, and say, "What more can *I* do?"

I encourage you to ask this question tonight. Journal it. Demand an answer. What more can I do to achieve the opportunities in front of me, to take back my health, to more fully celebrate the blessings God has granted me, to better love family members, to pay attention to those who maybe need a glimmer of hope?

Everything you do every day of your life matters profoundly.

When you chase success, your spark burns out quickly.

When you do something of significance, the spark jumps to life, spreads to others, and burns brightly long after you are gone.

The work you do quietly for others may not make headlines, but it will inspire others and give your life significance.

Decide today to make your family, your community, your organization, your world, a better place.

Pay attention.

Ask, "What more can I do?"

And see the spark catch flame and create a powerful inferno of change.

Choose significance.

**I wish I could show you . . .
the astonishing light of your own being.**

—HAFEZ

7

ARE YOU READY?

Fear and love are the two great motivators. While fear
suffocates, love liberates.

I *heard his voice outside my room.*

"*Is he ready?*"

Dad.

He was speaking to a nurse.

I didn't wait for her to answer.

I yelled from my room, "Yes! He is! Come and get him!"

Yeah, I was ready.

I sat in my wheelchair looking around the hospital room. It had
been my home for the last five months. The single window, little TV,
big bed with metal bars, calendar on the wall, yellow walls, bleachy
smell.

I wasn't going to miss it.

We were going home.

Home.

The big glass door slid open. I saw Dad enter the room.

He was pushing a wheelbarrow.

The wheelbarrow was overflowing with champagne and Life Savers candy. It was his present for all the nurses who had done so much for me. Looked like I wasn't going to be the only one who had a party today.

He pushed the wheelbarrow to my bedside, bent down, and kissed my cheek.

"Well, John?" he said. "What do you think? Are you ready for this?"

"This" meant a wheelchair ride to the elevator, down four flights, and out the front door to our station wagon. "This" meant no more blood technicians coming in early in the morning, no more days packed with therapy and bandage changes and bad food, no more nights spent missing my parents, listening to beeping, and longing for home. "This" meant leaving the hospital, going home, and having a party at our house with my parents, siblings, family, and friends.

I looked up at Dad, smiled, and told him I was definitely ready.

As we waited for the last discharge papers to be signed, he said, "Well, I just want you to know I'm proud of you. We all are. The doctors. The nurses. Everybody. You did it, you little monkey. You did it."

He paused.

"I am so proud of you. And I love you so much, John."

Those words.

They were almost exactly the same as the words he'd spoken five months earlier, words that saved my life.

Hearing them took me right back to that moment. . . .

After the ambulance had rushed me to the hospital, the paramedics had rolled me into a little waiting room. They pulled the curtain closed around me. A few nurses came in and checked on me. They told me it would all be okay, that everything would be fine.

Then they walked out of the room.

And I lay in the bed.

No one around.

All by myself.

I was scared and in pain and sad.

But mostly I just kept thinking about one thing.

I basically had one thought that morning.

My dad was going to freaking kill me when he found out what I'd done.

My dad hated when I didn't listen. When I ignored his rules.

I wasn't supposed to play with fire.

And that morning, I blew up his house.

I messed up bad.

The last time I'd messed up was two weeks earlier. It was a Sunday morning. I'd gone to church and then out to breakfast with my family.

After getting home, Dad told me to change before going outside to play.

But breakfast had taken forever.

I was already late meeting my friends.

So when the car had been parked in the driveway, and everyone else had gone inside, I snuck off to my buddy's house.

All my friends were already there, and we spent an afternoon playing tackle football.

It was an awesome day.

Until I got home and saw my dad.

I was sweaty.

Muddy.

Grass stains covered my church clothes.

He was not happy.

He grabbed my wrist, led me to my room, sat me on my bed, and told me how disappointed he was.

I kept my head down.

He asked if I knew it was a bad idea to play in my Sunday clothes.

I nodded.

He asked if I'd heard him say to change after we got home.

I nodded.

He asked why I hadn't listened.

I shrugged my shoulders.

He told me how disappointed he was in me and that it better never happen again.

He then walked out and closed the door.

I had to sit alone in that room thinking about what I'd done. For the entire night!

That was for ruining a pair of dress pants.

Now, I'd done something worse. Much worse.

Khaki pants ruined? Try blowing up the house.

I'd caused the fire.

I'd burned myself.

I'd ruined his house.

I'd put my family in danger.

My dad was going to freaking kill me.

Then, I heard his voice, like a lion, roaring down the hall.

"Where is my son, John O'Leary?"

Oh my gosh.

He'd found out.

And he was coming to finish me off.

A nurse down the hall did me no favors; she led him right back to where I was. I saw his shadow grow bigger through the curtain as he approached. I saw his arm dart forward; the curtain pulling back.

Don't let him kill me! Don't let him kill me! I thought as I prepared for his wrath.

But I was ready for it. And I deserved it.

He walked swiftly to my bed.

Then he spoke.

Gently.

"Hello, my little monkey!"

A smile appeared on his face.

I shut my eyes.

What the heck was going on?

Why was he being so nice?

Then he said, "John, look at me."

I opened my eyes and looked up at my dad.

"I have never been so proud of anyone in my entire life. Do you hear me?"

I looked away. What was he talking about?

He said it again, "Look at me, John. I love you so much. I love you."

I couldn't believe what he was saying.

I couldn't believe he wasn't mad.

And then it all started to make sense.

It all became clear.

I understood.

Nobody had told him what had happened!

That first day, that's how I felt. Oh, but Dad knew.

He knew.

And over the next five months in the hospital I thought often of that morning.

Of those words.

I never forgot what those words did for me.

And now, as Dad stood there, with a wheelbarrow full of candy, his eyes full of joy, I knew that he was the reason that this day had come. My dad saved my life.

And now, I was finally going home.

Before Jack Buck appeared.

Before the therapists stretched me.

Before Nurse Roy walked in.

Before the staff worked to save me.

Before Mom appeared and asked that extraordinary, inspired question.

Before anyone had a chance to do anything, the first person to visit me in the emergency room was Dad.

It was a mighty inflection point for him and for me.

Dad hadn't been told the extent of my injuries. Hadn't been warned about what he was about to step into. He just knew that I had been burned and was in the emergency room.

He rushed in, pulled back the curtain, and saw me lying there.

It would have taken the most seasoned health-care professional's breath away. He beheld his nine-year-old son, dwarfed by the adult-size hospital bed, bald, naked, and skinless. He saw his little boy alone, half-covered by a thin sheet, and whimpering.

Nothing could have prepared him for it.

His baby boy was going to die.

Fear flooded him. He felt paralyzed by it. What could he say? Why was this happening?

Then Dad saw past the wounds, pushed past the fear, beheld his son, and immediately stepped in with love.

Daringly, faithfully, lovingly, he cut through his fear, shock, and sadness, came directly to me, leaned over, and smiled. He told me he was proud of me. And told me he loved me.

I love you.

Three simple words that changed my world.

And they can change yours.

THE SHIFT

Dad wasn't the only one paralyzed by fear.

It's absurd looking back on it, but in that moment I wasn't scared of dying. All I could think about was how badly I'd let Dad down, hurt my family, damaged my house, and ruined my life.

I thought my entire family would be furious. And I honestly thought my dad was going to kill me.

Think back to when you were a kid. Did you ever do anything stupid? Ever let your family down? Remember how they reacted after you came home with a bad report card? Or after you broke a window playing ball? Or arrived home after your curfew?

Okay. You got in trouble for that stuff, right?

They were mad at you, right?

Try blowing up their house this weekend.

Let's see how they react to *that* one.

That certainly was what I was anticipating.

But in reality, all those moments I spent terrified of my dad were wasted.

That's often the case with fear.

Perhaps Mark Twain said it best: "I have been through some terrible things in my life, some of which actually happened."

Think about that for a moment.

Fear is rooted in what *may* happen, something that does not even exist in reality. Yet how frequently we allow this emotion to consume our thoughts, ultimately deciding the course of our lives.

But Dad knew better.

It may seem simple, but when Dad let go of his fear and stepped into the situation with love, his words served as a warm light, cutting through the darkness I'd been in all morning. Those words brought me from a place with no chance to one where I could take the next breath and fight forward. Those words empowered me moments later when Dad left the room, and Mom entered and asked, "Do you want to die?"

No, Mom. I want to live.

I want to live.

Before Dad came in that morning I was stuck in total despair and wanted to die. I was suffocating in fear.

After he left, I had a glimmer of hope and a strong desire to live.

I was saved by love.

And it can save us all.

I'll let Pedro Arrupe explain:

What you are in love with . . . will affect everything. It will decide what will get you out of bed in the morning, . . . how you spend your weekends, what you read, . . . what breaks your heart and what amazes you with joy and gratitude. Fall in love, stay in love, and it will decide everything.

That is a beautiful sentiment about the power of love. It affects everything.

But now reread the quote supplanting the word *love* with the word *fear*. Go ahead, do it now. Replace the word *love* with the word *fear* and read it again.

What you fear . . . will affect everything. It will decide what will get you out of bed in the morning, . . . how you spend your weekends, what you read, . . . what breaks your heart and what amazes you with joy and gratitude. Fall into fear, stay in fear, and it will decide everything.

The quote still reads accurately.

Whether you choose to be seized by love or fear will affect everything that happens in your life.

Fall in love, stay in love, and it will decide everything.

Fall into fear, stay in fear, and it will decide everything.

NICE TO MEET YOU

The first time I met Beth's family, I received advice I'll never forget.

It was nearly Christmas and we were ushering in the holidays with a large family party. Beth and I had been dating for just a couple months, and it was time to meet her family. There were several dozen uncles, aunts, and cousins. The gathering was loud, full of laugher, food, drink, and good cheer. I felt at home immediately.

Near the end of the party I got to spend some time with one of their older family friends. Though an older man, he still had a square jaw, buzz cut, large, powerful hands, and a spark of mischief in his eyes. We were standing in his house, near the kitchen table, laden with food.

He leaned over to grab another cookie, took a bite, then said, "Do you know what I do when I meet someone for the first time, John?"

No, sir. Tell me.

"Well, John, I always turn sideways."

He turned sideways.

"I cock my left hand."

He made a tight fist.

"That way I am ready in case the person tries to swing at me. I can swing, hit him first, and drop him."

There was an awkward silence.

"Do you understand?"

He kept eating the cookie as I nodded yes. Eyeing that left fist of his, I asked, *So you're saying that every time you meet someone for the first time you're ready for a fight?*

"That's right. And I'd drop him to the ground. There would be nothing he could do about it. Just nothing he could do about it."

He wasn't sharing this statement as a way to intimidate me, but instead as some advice he considered valuable. Now, this was an amazing man, wonderful friend, and we miss his sweetness and idiosyncrasies.

But he grew up in a tough neighborhood, lived during the Depression, had fought in a war, and the residue of those experiences shaped every new encounter he faced.

Can you imagine going through life that way? Can you imagine every time you meet someone making a fist, getting ready to throw down? Can you imagine every time you shake someone's hand you have your left hand clenched, ready to swing?

It's outrageous.

But while we may laugh at this story, most of us are more like him than we'd like to admit.

We occasionally start our day with our fists clenched, ready to throw down. We sometimes greet others with our shields up, masks on, prepared for war. We can become used to greeting adversity and opportunity, the ordinary and the extraordinary, the sunshine and the rainstorms—not with an open heart on fire with love, but with one frozen shut by fear.

Now, fear can be a good thing.

We should fear touching something hot, letting someone down, a hungry lion. In my faith, even the fear of God is a good thing as it propels believers away from something destructive and toward something life-giving.

Fear is part of our human experience and necessary for our survival.

The goal, though, is not to stay in a fear-based mentality. If we dwell in a place of fear, we'll never get anywhere.

MY SISTER

I was getting ready to leave.

After five months in the hospital it was time to go out into the world again. Everyone was celebrating the miracle. My parents were overjoyed at the prospect of my homecoming. My dad leaned over one afternoon, days before my release, put a hand on my shoulder, looked into my eyes, and said, "John, everything is going to work out fine."

From my wheelchair, still connected to a heart monitor and a feeding tube and wrapped with bandages, I looked up at him. I must have been having a bit of a bad day because I remember responding:

That's easy for you to say, I huffed. *You've got a wife, a family, a job, and a home. I may never have those things.*

I was a passionate, precocious, courageous little guy. But at some moments in my childhood, after the fire, I was dominated by fear. Afraid of what people might say. Afraid of what I might not be able to do. And most definitely afraid that I would never have what everyone seemed to be striving for . . . a job, a wife, a home, and a family.

I was afraid I was never going to have the chance.

Fearful I was never going to find real love.

Scared that I'd never have a normal life.

That anxiety stayed with me as I aged. I attended DeSmet Jesuit High School, an all-boys school (thanks Mom and Dad, not doing me any favors here!). But I still developed some friendships with girls from the local Catholic girls school.

Even went to a few homecoming dances.

But it was always as "just friends."

I played it cool and acted as if I didn't care. Lots of guys made it to college without being kissed. No big deal. I was sure something would happen in college.

But deep down I was afraid. I'd look down at my hands. And curse that they'd had to take my fingers.

Because despite that I could write, drive a car, shoot baskets, throw a baseball . . . I had no idea how I would ever hold hands with a girl.

No one was going to want me.

This fear was echoing through my head as I entered college. The pattern continued through my freshman, sophomore, and junior years. Lots of friends, no girlfriends, the gentle companion of fear whispering, *It's just not meant to be.*

Then it all changed.

I met *the one.*

At a party second semester junior year I saw her across the room.

She was absolutely stunning.

Brunette, with big brown eyes and a bright, beautiful smile, she looked like Jackie Kennedy or Julia Roberts . . . only prettier.

I asked who she was and learned she was a freshman named Elizabeth Grace Hittler. I walked over to her, introduced myself, and we talked for a while. I asked if she wanted to dance and began to drag her onto the dance floor before she could even respond. We danced to my favorite Neil Diamond song, "Sweet Caroline." We had a blast, hung out the entire night, and I knew I had just met my future wife.

But as the night drew to a close, I started second-guessing myself. Why would she want to date me? What if my hands repulsed her, let alone the scars that covered my body? What if she discovered how far from perfect I actually was?

I decided not to ask her out.

Why risk the rejection?

Fear slammed that door shut.

We went our separate ways that night. But we became close friends over time. I spent an entire year getting to know her, letting her know me, and hoping against all odds we might end up together. As the year progressed, our friendship strengthened, my emotions toward her intensified, and I knew I just had to ask her out.

I was ready.

So at a social function on campus, I pulled Beth aside, left behind all the hesitation, all the fear, and all the apprehensions, and boldly put myself out there.

By this time I knew she'd say yes. That's why it had taken me so long to ask; I needed to be sure she'd say yes first.

I figured she'd respond, "What took so long?!"

I was far from ready when she looked into my eyes, smiled sweetly, and said, "John, you are like a brother to me."

Now, I don't know what you've heard about Missouri.

But it's not true.

This was her way of saying *no*!

This was her way of letting me know, as thoughtfully as she could, that she wasn't interested, that there wasn't a chance, and that there was never going to be a chance.

I defused the situation with a lame attempt at humor. I told her I always wanted another sister. I hoped she'd forget it ever happened. But deep down her rejection crushed me.

This was the first time I'd really put myself out there. Her rejection brought back those fears of a nine-year-old. Would I always have to be alone? What if the scars bound me not only to a painful experience from the past, but a life alone in the future? What if having a bunch of sisters was about as good as I was ever going to get?

Another year passed.

We stayed friends.

Yet, my feelings for her remained.

Sensing that they were beginning to be reciprocated, I told Beth that my feelings for her hadn't changed. I told her I was still strongly attracted to her; that the last year of getting to know her made me like her even more.

There was a long silence as she looked back at me.

Dang, she had an awesome poker face.

And she was absolutely beautiful.

Then she spoke.

"John, nothing has changed. I love you and think you're great. But as a friend, more like a brother."

Seriously. Didn't she know by now I already had four freaking sisters? I didn't need another one!

I laugh about this story now. But as a young man, already unsure of himself and his future, this was truly crushing.

I was sick of giving away everything I had. I was sick of being judged by hands and scars that I could not change. I was sick of trying. And I was sick of failing.

C. S. Lewis writes, "To love at all is to be vulnerable. Love anything, and your heart will certainly be wrung and possibly broken. If you want to make sure of keeping it intact, you must give your heart to no one, not even to an animal. Wrap it carefully round with hobbies and little luxuries; avoid all entanglements; lock it up safe in the casket or coffin of your selfishness. But in that casket—safe, dark, motionless, airless—it will change. It will not be broken; it will become unbreakable, impenetrable, irredeemable."

I was ready for my heart to be unbreakable.

Impenetrable.

Irredeemable.

I was done.

Done with Beth.

Done with dating.

Done with rejection.

Done with love.

TRUE LOVE

This is a place we all find ourselves at times in our lives.

Hosting a pity party. Feeling painfully alone, broken in disappointment, with only negative thoughts as company. But haven't you ever noticed that it's the only party that no one else ever attends with you?

It's a gathering with room for only one.

When you're all alone, the voice of fear can overwhelm. It can begin to feel like the only thing that's real. When we spend too much time concerned only about ourselves, the inner voice in our head begins to echo, doesn't it? Reverberating from side to side to side, the voice grows louder each time.

The echo of fear silences opportunity.

Ah, but love can break open the echo chamber.

Fear is a cage where we feel totally confined, but faith is the key that sets us free. So I began praying about, reflecting on, and journaling about what it meant to be in love. I began to wonder, *What does a successful, significant, joy-filled life even look like?* And I began considering what I'd really been wanting from Beth—or any relationship—in life.

It didn't take long before I realized that my desire had been selfish.

I was transfixed on what that relationship, and to be honest, most relationships, might do for me. I was so focused on what I wanted. I wanted Beth to be my date, my girlfriend, my wife, my security, even my proof that I was normal. But in focusing everything on my desires for the relationship, I was unable to just enjoy who Beth was and the wonderful relationship we had.

I decided I had to stop trying to convince her that I was lovable.

I let go of my fear that I would always be alone.

I opened the door of my heart and loved her even though it wasn't exactly the way I had planned.

In doing so I unlocked the seventh choice to ignite a radically inspired life: choose to let go of fear and operate, lead, and live from a place of unconditional love.

It was a mighty inflection point.

When we were out together, I stopped worrying about me. The focus shifted to actually caring about her. Instead of me trying to get anything from the relationship, I began to just enjoy whatever time we had together. Instead of focusing on dating or desires, the focus shifted to simply loving her and enjoying the moment.

No strings attached. No expectations. No hidden agenda.

And it was enough.

It was more than enough. It was awesome.

On a cool September night, though, that changed again.

Beth and I were at a wonderful Italian restaurant (Italian is her favorite kind of food), sitting on the patio (my favorite place to sit). Shortly after ordering she leaned over to me and said she had something to tell me.

She then took a sip of her wine.

No, let me be more accurate: she took a mighty gulp.

She said that over the past six months, every time she'd see me, she'd get butterflies in her stomach. She didn't know why they were there and sometimes wished they'd fly away. But they hadn't.

There was silence.

She then looked me in the eye.

"John, what I'm trying to say is . . . I've fallen for you. Is it too late? Or would you be interested in . . . dating?"

I was shocked.

I didn't expect it and didn't know how to respond.

So I looked Beth in her eyes and told her as sweetly as I could, *Sorry, Beth. I don't date sisters.*

Now.

Do you really think that's what I said?!

No, I drooled out the words:

Yes! Let's try this, Beth!

Well, we tried it.

Three years later, we were married.

We have an incredible marriage. No marriage, no relationship, is without some challenges. We are dealing with the same complexities and compromises of any other couple. We get squirrels in our attic, ants in our kitchen, and water in our basement. We have occasional trials with our kids, constant pulls on time, and even occasional arguments.

But nothing worthy is easy.

We're deeply committed to one another, share a strong faith, and remain totally in love with each other. She's an incredible mom. We have four healthy kids that range in age from four to ten. She faces continuous demands to drive car pool, help with homework, mend bloody knees, mitigate yelling, break up fighting, clean little bodies, wash dirty clothes, get the kids tucked in, prayed up, and in bed. She does it every single day whether I'm on the road for business or not, and I could not do what I do without the effort and love she invests each day.

And every single time I'm with Beth or any of my four favorite little ones, I am overwhelmed with gratitude. They were absolutely worth the wait.

True love always is worth the wait.

THE NUMBER ONE FAILURE INDICATOR

I look back on my life and wonder what would have happened if I had stayed in my fearful, self-focused mind-set. What if I'd not let go of that fear and not opened myself up to what real love, and the grandeur of real life, looked like?

I most certainly would not be where I am today.

You see, fear is the number one thing holding us back.

If we don't conquer fear, we can't live a radically inspired life.

Think about it.

Everything put forward in this book, the seven choices to ignite a radically inspired life, are easily squelched and smothered by fear.

Fear keeps you from being *accountable*. How much easier to wait for someone else to solve things, step forward, take responsibility? Fear suffocates possibility by nudging you forward with the expression "It's not your fault . . . it's never your fault."

Fear keeps you from fully *embracing your story*. It silences your ability to be, celebrate, and share who you really are. It encourages you to keep that mask held high.

Fear keeps you from going *All In*. It keeps you from risking greatly and impacting profoundly. It whispers to hold back in case something goes wrong.

Fear keeps you locked in victim mentality. It makes having gratitude and rejoicing in the great gifts of each day impossible. It murmurs that you should blame others, wallow in pity, and sink in despair.

Fear keeps you from growing and stretching. It makes continual improvements and advances in your relationships, business, and life implausible. It makes us feel it's easier to stay where things are comfortable.

Fear keeps you focused on yourself. It makes true significance, true success, and truly selfless living an absolute impossibility. Fear reminds you that it's a dog-eat-dog world, and to take care of your needs, your interests, and your desires first.

Fear keeps you stuck right where you are, worried about the what-ifs, the oh-nos, the what-can-I-dos. It keeps your arms crossed, your armor up, and your fist clenched.

There's another way.

There always is.

What if you could walk into every interaction expecting a smile, a new friend, and a true connection? What if every moment was seen as a miracle? What if each interaction was seen not from the perspective of what might go wrong next, but from one certain that the best is yet to come?

Fear.

Or love.

It's a choice.

What will you choose?

JOIN THE SYMPHONY

Scars last a lifetime.

They may fade a bit in time, they may decrease a bit in size, but they never fully disappear. Mine are so thick that they sometimes get infected. These abscesses form deep within the scar tissue.

It starts with a low-grade fever, slight achiness in my body, and general soreness in the area of the infection. Within a day the fever climbs, my body aches, it becomes difficult to even get out of bed, and the area around the growing infection throbs.

When I was a kid, somehow Mom was able to detect an infection in the look on my face, the way I walked, or how I was acting.

That bloodhoundlike capability of detecting these darn things has now been effectively passed down to my wife. Beth sometimes knows I have them before I realize it.

Just a few months after our wedding, Beth was getting ready for work. I was dragging a bit, still in bed and under the covers. Despite my telling her everything was fine, she sensed something was wrong. She sat down on the bed, stroked my hair, and asked if I had another sore.

I didn't answer.

Pulling up my T-shirt, she saw a substantial skin infection growing on my stomach. These things are brutal. They cause the entire area around them to turn bright red. The abscesses can protrude out from the stomach more than an inch and spread in diameter several inches. They're painful to endure and terribly ugly to see.

Beth asked what she could do for me.

I asked for an ice water, some medicine, and for her to start my bathwater. The warm water reduces the throbbing pain. She disappeared, and I heard the bathwater run. Moments later she came back carrying a glass of ice water and some medicine. She set them down and sat back on the bed with me.

She gently pulled up my T-shirt again. Looked down at the red lesion. Then looked at me and said, "I hate these things. But I love you."

She then bent over and gently kissed the sore. Pulling my shirt back down, she told me to call her if I needed anything during the day.

Now, was this a Herculean act?

No.

But those of you who've been in pain and just wanted someone to acknowledge it and share it with you understand the power of that kiss. That part of me that I hated most, she blessed with a kiss.

Did she have to kiss that gross, painful scar?

No.

But she wanted to.

She didn't have to, she wanted to.

What are the words we exchange on the altar?

I do.

Frequently those two words that originated in love shift through the years to three words based in fear: *I have to.*

It's a cancerous shift.

And we all face that choice many times throughout the day.

Do something out of obligation, out of fear, out of *I have to.*

Or do it out of joy, out of love, out of *I want to.*

Think about it for a moment. *Wanting* to do something is so much more liberating than *having* to do something. *I have to* is wrapped up in the fear of what might happen if you don't perform the way you're supposed to. *I want to* is a beautiful gift to anyone around you.

The tension and stress associated with *I have to* go to work, forgive her, move forward, watch my weight, clean my house, pick up the kids, be home for dinner, dissipates when the sentence begins with *I want to.*

Just try it.

I *want* to clean my house means you look forward to how beautiful it will look when finished, the joy people will have when they come into it, the sense of accomplishment you will feel when the work is done.

Or I *have* to clean my house. Just one more dreary task that makes up the drudgery of your life.

I *want* to be home for dinner means you can't wait to see your family, anticipate the delicious food you might enjoy together, the chance to talk about your day.

Or I *have* to be home for dinner—it becomes an annoyance, you wish you could get more done at work, you wish you could stay for one more drink, you begrudgingly pack your bag and head home, annoyed at this thing you are supposed to do.

It's just one word.

But it makes all the difference.

Being motivated by love sets you free. There is no obligation. There's only joy. It's no longer about you. It can instead be about others. And let me tell you, when you turn outward in love, you create the kind of joy that spreads like wildfire.

Did Jack Buck *have* to help me, or all those other people when he stepped into their lives in little ways?

Nope. But he sure *wanted* to.

Did Glenn Cunningham *have* to take in nine thousand kids?

Nope. But he sure *wanted* to.

Did Nurse Roy *have* to promise me that I'd walk again?

Nope. But he sure *wanted* to.

This is the final choice that makes all the difference, that allows you to start living a radically inspired life.

THERE'S NOTHING YOU CAN DO ABOUT IT

Here's the secret.

If you are going to transform your life from a series of obligations to a long list of moments for joy, then you have to learn the secret.

Love is not just reserved for our inner circle. Our friends and family. It is intended to be the currency of our world. Offered to everyone you meet.

Let me explain.

All day long we get to choose how we approach each moment.

We are free to live out of fear: How is this guy going to take advantage of me? I better cock my fist. Or I better keep my guard up, this guy might steal my account. Or, okay, I'm already running late, I'm going to cut people off, walk with my head down, and make life all about me. My needs. My wants. My life. Me.

Fear, frustration, annoyance, before we've even given anyone a chance.

But we hold the power to open the doors to possibility just as my dad did that morning in the ER.

So, are you ready for the secret?

It's a phrase you say in your head to every person you meet.

You're not going to like it.

How do I know that?

Because here's what happens when I share this secret in my presentations.

"Turn to the person next to you and say, 'Hi.'"

No matter how big or small the group, everyone knows how to do this part. So I hear a hearty chorus of "Hi."

"Really well done. Now say these words: 'Um, this is awkward for me, too.'"

People laugh and say those words.

"Awesome! You're doing great! Here's the next one: 'I love you, and there's nothing you can do about it!'"

Awkward pause. People shift in seats.

"All right," I say, "let's try that again. 'I love you, and there's nothing you can do about it!'"

Slowly, people begin to murmur the phrase.

What is it about our culture that we are so uncomfortable expressing love? Why is it something that we hold back tightly, as if it were a precious commodity and if you give it away, you'll never get it back?

You see, love multiplies.

So here's where I have to push people.

"Aw, come on. What was that? Is that really how you tell someone you love them? Say it loud, with conviction! *I love you, and there's nothing you can do about it!*"

Finally, people jump All In. The room erupts in laughter. I feel the change immediately. People put down their armor, let go of their ego, and start to realize that approaching anyone, even a total stranger, through a lens of love is possible, powerful, and a gift to all involved.

This exercise isn't just something to make people laugh. It isn't something I'd recommend using as a pickup line at a bar.

No. Come on. You're better than that! But it is something to consider: What if we approached each situation in our lives through the lens of love rather than the lens of fear?

Your spouse in the morning: I love you, and there's nothing you can do about it!

The person cutting in front of you in rush-hour traffic: I love you, and there's nothing you can do about it!

The disengaged operator on the phone: I love you, and there's nothing you can do about it!

Your difficult coworker at the office: I love you, and there's nothing you can do about it!

The mom on the other side of the playground glaring at your child: I love you, and there's nothing you can do about it!

Those words allow you to focus on others, on their needs and on what they are saying. It keeps you mindful of what they might need in that moment, instead of what they might take from you; or what you might get from them. And it keeps you focused on the present, on the possibility that dwells within this redolent and holy moment.

This pause, and those words, can also be used for you. Those words allow you to focus on the most important person, by far, in your life: you. They empower you to breathe life and possibility into each of your moments. They permit you to take time for yourself, for your health, for your spirit. Because if you can't first take care of yourself, it's difficult, perhaps impossible, to effectively encourage and serve others in their lives.

I love you drops your barriers, then theirs.

It allows you to achieve mighty things by focusing on the little things.

When you do that, your life can become a series of I-want-tos, a symphony of joy.

Let the music begin.

DAD GETS THE CALL

Can I borrow the car?

It's a question every kid asks of his or her parents. My senior year of college I asked it of Dad.

It was spring break, my friends were going skiing, and we needed a reliable car to get us through the snow we were sure to encounter. Dad had just bought a new Toyota 4Runner. It had a CD player, leather seats, a sunroof, and less than a thousand miles on it. It had four-wheel drive. Perfect.

Dad dropped off his beautiful taupe vehicle and picked up my beat-up clunker. I hugged him and thanked him. I promised to be careful. I then loaded up his car, picked up a college friend, and headed to Colorado to meet up with the rest of our group.

We left at dusk.

Snow started falling around midnight halfway across Kansas.

Near the Colorado border I pulled over, too tired to drive any farther. My friend, bright eyed and lit up with coffee, took over behind the wheel. He assured me he wasn't tired and was ready to roll.

I shut my eyes.

Ten minutes later I awoke when my head was slammed into the passenger-side-door window.

Rob had lost control of the car. The car, hurtling uncontrollably down the highway, fishtailed hard into the barricade to the left, spun 360 degrees, crossed back over the highway, hit the guardrail on the right, bounced off, and spun us around one more time. We came to a stop . . . facing the oncoming traffic.

Physically, we were both fine. But the car refused to start. The lights from the massive eighteen-wheelers loomed toward us. Then around us, the trucks blaring their horns, enveloping us with snow as they passed.

"We've got to move this car!" I shouted. My whole body was practically paralyzed with fear. *How were we going to get out of this?*

"The only way is to get out and push, I think," Rob said, his face showing he had no desire to do this either. But to sit where we were meant to stay in a death trap.

We got out of the car and painstakingly pushed the vehicle through the snow, off the highway, onto the shoulder, out of danger. It was frigid. It was the middle of the night, in the middle of nowhere. The wind howled, the snow fell, but at least we were off the highway.

We got back in the car for warmth. But even the car was getting cold.

After we repeatedly turned the key to no avail, the engine finally kicked on. I put the car in drive, turned it to face the proper direction, and started slowly down the highway. We limped down the road; the bumper dragged against the pavement and fenders rubbed against both front tires. We were in eastern Colorado, civilization seemed far from us, and we remained concerned about being stranded.

After cautiously driving several miles we saw dim lights in the distance. An oasis, a small town, hope. We wobbled toward the light, then off the highway, into town, and found a hotel.

We checked in around 3:30 a.m.

Went upstairs.

Fell into our respective beds.

My friend started snoring almost immediately.

I just lay there, heart pounding, mind racing.

I didn't sleep that night.

It wasn't the concern over what had happened. It wasn't in gratitude for the two guardrails that had kept us from disappearing off the road and into the night. It wasn't how cold my body still felt from that bone-chilling air.

No.

What kept me up was the thought of calling Dad and telling him what had happened.

The 4Runner was brand new. I had promised to be careful with it. And now I was going to have to let him know it was mangled up in some little Colorado town. I adore both my parents and don't enjoy letting them down. I hated the idea of betraying their trust.

At 6:00 a.m. I left the room, went to the lobby, grabbed a coffee, and called Dad.

He's a morning person and answered cheerfully, "Hello."

I took a long sip of coffee, a deep breath, then shared, *Hi, Dad. Rob and I are fine, but we were in a car accident last night in Colorado.*

"Are you okay?"

Yeah, Dad, but your car is really banged up. I feel horrible. You let us take—

"Listen, John. The car isn't a problem. That's easy to fix. I'm just glad that you guys are okay. Do you need help getting another car?"

We'll figure it out, Dad.

"You sure you are okay?"

Yeah. Totally fine. Just feel bad this happened. I'm so sorry. I'm going to make it up to you. When we get home, I'm going to—

"John. The car can be fixed. Have it towed, get a rental, and be careful skiing. Have fun. I love you."

I love you, too.

We hung up.

That was it.

The massive concern I had regarding Dad's wrath was misplaced.

Again.

He had responded with love.

Again.

I love you, and there's nothing you can do about it!

Although those exact words didn't come out of his mouth, that was the sentiment Dad was expressing when he said he didn't care about the car, he just wanted to make sure I was okay. It was what he was saying when he came to me all those years ago in the hospital and said I love you. *You blew up my garage, almost killed yourself, we can't live in the house for months, but I love you. I love you, and there's nothing you can do to take it away.*

It is the sentiment I see lived out in Beth as she greets me, smiles at me, loves me even as my travel intensifies. I get home exhausted, and I am far from perfect. *I love you, and there's nothing you can do about it!* And it's certainly what I see from her as we raise our little ones . . . although they frequently try testing that love!

Love gives you a laserlike focus on what is truly important.

Without it, we are frozen in the dark.

With it, we light up the world.

MIRACLES HAPPEN

Love is the greatest power on earth.

And that amazing power was about to shine brightly again.

Almost two decades after Dad saw me in the emergency room at St. John's Mercy, I had to call him from that same hospital. It was just after 2:00 a.m. on November 14, 2005. I called home and woke Dad. I'd never been through anything like this before and needed him there as soon as possible. I knew he would reach over, wake my mom, get dressed, and hop in the car as fast as he could.

Less than an hour later, I heard his familiar voice outside our room: "Where's my son John?"

I knew he'd come.

And I knew how he'd react.

Finally, at this point in my life, I knew Dad.

I knew love.

He entered the room, walked over to where Beth was lying in the hospital bed, and kissed her cheek.

Then he came over to where I sat in a chair.

He looked down at me.

His eyes filled with tears.

He bent down.

Looked into my eyes.

Stared fixedly.

Then spoke.

Gently.

"John, I love you so much, and I am so proud of you."

He then leaned forward and kissed the velvety fuzz on the top of my healthy newborn son Jack's head.

I beamed up at Dad, my eyes also full of tears and my heart full of pride.

I knew that he was thinking of how far I had come. That he, too, remembered my fears before I left the hospital.

And here I was, all these years later, holding my son.

I was a father myself.

It was a miracle.

Where he had once walked into this hospital facing every

parent's worst nightmare, today we were walking into every parent's dream.

We had come so far.

Staff, siblings, parents, celebrities, family, friends, and strangers worked for it.

A little boy had fought for it.

God had orchestrated it.

And love had fueled it.

What an amazing, inspiring, liberating force to celebrate. It's not just for your spouse and kids, your mom and dad. It's not just an emotion reserved for your favorite sports team, television show, or vacation spot.

No, it's a lens through which you can view life.

And when you do, life becomes a series of opportunities, a progression of miracles, and you can go through life not like a bitter old man, scared of what might be around every corner, but like a bright-eyed, bushy-tailed kid, in love with life.

Are you ready to join me?

FEAR V. LOVE

*I will love the light for it shows me the way, yet I will endure the
darkness for it shows me the stars.*
—Og Mandino

There is a myth that love is soft.

The truth is, sometimes love is hard. Love takes action. It's not a fuzzy
feeling. Love is a verb, it's unselfish, and it propels you into doing
something, usually something for someone else. You see, fear is always
selfish. It's concerned with what you can get, what you need, what might
happen to you.

Love? It's always about others.

And in truly caring for others we are taken care of, too.

Here's your inflection point: fear or love? I have to or I want to?

You only have one life to live. Do you want to lead it cowering in fear,
stressed by things that might never happen, hiding from the possibilities
that lurk around every corner? Living in the *I have to* mentality?

Or do you want to wake each day energized with possibility, knowing
that you hold the power to change your life, and the lives of others,
by living each day on fire with love? Eager to see what is around each
corner? Ready to take life by the reins?

Every day we can choose: Shut people out or open our hearts; clench our
fists or open up our arms? The choice we make can transform lives.

Starting with our own.

You see, when you let go of fear, your hands can finally grasp the love
and joy that have been waiting all along.

Choose love.

AWAKENING

Don't confuse being out of bed with being fully awake.

G*ot an awesome gift today.*

And I needed it.

Two weeks ago the doctors performed skin grafts on my back.

Since then I've been stuck lying on my tummy because I can't put pressure on my back.

Fourteen days looking down through a hole they cut in the bed.

Fourteen days of staring at the same gray tile.

But then he came in.

I'm a huge hockey fan. And Gino Cavallini is a hockey player with the St. Louis Blues. He's been visiting me for about a month. He's really cool.

Today he walked in.

Got down on his knees.

Looked up through the hole they cut in the mattress.

Smiled at me.

"How you doing, Superstar?"

I was in pain, tied to a bed, staring through a hole, barely able to speak, and it's been like this for a couple weeks. So I said, "Awesome."

But I think he could tell I didn't mean it.

"Superstar, in tonight's game I'm going to do something for you. I'm going to score a goal for you."

Now, I love hockey.

I follow all of the Blues games.

And I know a lot about Gino.

He's more of a tough guy than a goal scorer.

And I didn't want him to disappoint himself . . . or me.

I looked at him through the hole. Looked into his eyes and said, "Gino, do us both a favor. Get in a fight instead, man."

For some reason he laughed.

Gino looked up at me. He was still kneeling on the floor. He kept smiling and said, "All right, Superstar! You got it. In tonight's game if I can't score a goal, I promise I'll get in a fight!"

We talked for a little longer.

Then he left to get ready for the game.

That night, Mom and Dad sat next to each other at the head of my bed. We listened to the hockey game.

Instead of staring at the floor, I just shut my eyes and imagined I was at the game. On the radio, hockey is a little like listening to an auctioneer . . . it's fast paced, it's exciting, but you aren't always sure what the heck is going on.

But then it happened!

Near the end of the first period, with the score tied 1–1, my friend Gino Cavallini kept his promise!

He actually did it!

There was a massive brawl near center ice.

Gino had dropped his gloves; he was in a fight.

I grinned ear to ear thinking about him tangled up with one of the bad guys, taking care of business for me!

I knew he could do it!

For a while I floated in that bed. Couldn't believe he actually did it! Wow, wait until my buddies hear about this. Gino got in a fight. For me!

Gino went to the penalty box for fighting, but the game continued.

And we kept listening.

Near the end of the game, Gino gave me another gift.

The score was tied 2–2.

Time was running out.

Then I heard the announcer start yelling with excitement.

A loud foghorn shrieked out over his voice.

They blast that horn whenever we score.

The announcer barked out that the Blues had just pulled ahead 3–2.

The go-ahead goal was scored by Gino Cavallini.

Now, teams always celebrate after a goal.

The announcer said there were high fives, hugs, and . . . tears.

But this was kind of weird for a hockey game.

Anyway, I knew Gino didn't score a lot, but I couldn't figure out how he and all the other players could be so excited to actually cry about it.

Mom said something about being overwhelmed with joy . . . something about the goal being much bigger than just a hockey game . . . something about a goal shared by the entire team that night . . . a goal for me to keep fighting forward.

I didn't know about all that.

I was just glad he got in a fight.

When the game ended, I settled in to go to sleep.

Hours later I heard a ruckus in the hallway.

Hockey players love to celebrate victories. And they usually celebrate at bars.

But that night was different.

Gino, his St. Louis Blues teammates, and a seven-foot, blue mascot went out together to celebrate their victory.

They picked up a couple dozen pizzas.

They grabbed a bunch of soda.

They made their way to a hospital parking lot.

They took the elevator to the fourth floor.

And they came to the burn center to party.

Mom came in, got down on her knees, and gently tapped my shoulder to wake me up.

She said, "There are some guys from the game who want to see you."

Gino walked in.

His arms were full.

He had a plate of pizza, a big cup of soda, the stick he scored with that night, and a seven-foot-tall, blue stuffed animal.

That night we partied.

We partied until almost two in the morning.

The nurses eventually kicked Gino and his friends out.

Before he left, Gino got down on his knees.

He looked up through the hole in the bed.

He smiled and asked, "How you doing now, Superstar?"

I looked at my friend.

Smiled.

And responded:

"Awesome."

We were on a train platform.

The three boys were near the edge, heads turned to the left, staring off to the west. They were excitedly waiting for the next train to arrive in the station. Their little sister was nestled in my arms, curious about what her brothers were so worked up about.

It was a chilly, lazy Saturday morning and we were on an adventure. My kids and I were taking the train from where we live, into the city to grab lunch downtown, and then, the grand finale, to go up in the Gateway Arch. After several days of traveling I needed a little Dad time with my babies. And after almost a week solo-parenting the four kids, my amazing wife probably wasn't too disappointed to have a little time without them.

One of my boys practically sang out, "Oh my gosh, I think it's coming! Yes, it is! Guys, it's here!"

I ordered the kids back from the tracks as the train raced into the station.

My three little boys practically leaped from the platform, through the open doorway, and onto the train. They were lit up!

We found a spot near the back of the train and made ourselves at home.

The train was full. Some passengers had their eyes shut, a few thumbed around, transfixed by their phones, while others blankly stared out the window. They endured the ride and awaited their stop. Tired. Bored. Surviving.

Then, there were my kids.

It was their first time on a train. They were beaming and enthusiastically pointed out every landmark we passed, widened their eyes at every tunnel we traveled through, and yelled every time we crossed a bridge. These four kids were fired up for the ride.

Excited.

Awake.

Alive.

Awesome.

They were on fire.

Why was the experience so different for them?

It was the same train.

Same ride.

Same landmarks.

Same exit for many of us.

And yet, it was a totally different experience for the typical passengers compared to my kids.

Why?

The easy answer is that they're kids, it was their first time, and the first time is always memorable.

But there is more to it than that.

My kids were fully awake. They knew that they were having an adventure. And they didn't want to miss a moment.

Sadly, we quickly lose that enthusiasm as adults, as our lives become a series of tasks, and we learn to go through the motions, barely noticing what is in front of us. We're sleepwalking. The great adventure of life mellows.

Ah, but it wasn't always so. Do you remember that intense feeling of anticipation when you did something for the first time?

The older we get, the further away those moments seem.

But dig deep into your memory.

A first day of school.

The first time behind a wheel.

A first kiss, first dance, first performance.

For a moment, you were totally alive, completely connected, fully present. You were totally in that moment; you were on fire with anticipation, excitement, life.

Ah, but then came the second day of school, the second kiss, another dance.

And then the third.

Before long, that excitement fades, and life becomes a series of been-there, done-that experiences. Enthusiasm saps out. Boredom seeps in.

But it doesn't have to be that way.

Can we learn to live every day fully alive? Fully engaged? First-time living?

Of course you know my answer by now.

PICTURE THIS

I have a bulletin board of letters hanging in my office.

On it hang several hundred notes sent from clients, audience members, and friends. The letters come from kids, executives, inmates, nurses, salespeople, patients, truck drivers, and schoolteachers. They remind me that my work matters and to keep striving forward.

I also have works of art and photos displayed.

There's one of a lineman working high on an electric pole. It reminds me of my work with Southern Company and Alabama Power—and their beautiful gift of reconnecting me to Nurse Roy. There's a painting of Jack Buck. He's broadcasting a game from behind a microphone. There're several crayon drawings I find particularly valuable from young artists who all share the last name O'Leary . . . and live in my house.

And then there is my favorite picture.

Taken in a hospital room, a picture of an older woman and me.

She is in bed.

From the looks of it she's been in bed a long time. She is speaking to me, seemingly sternly. I am listening, seemingly intently. But a huge grin is also on my face.

Her name was Sister Gertrude. I met her in preparing to give a presentation to the leaders of SSM Health. Because I wanted to meet the nuns who helped begin the hospital and first lived the mission, I visited the retirement center where many of those nuns now resided.

I came in and Sister Gertrude asked me to sit. She told me to pull the chair right next to the bed.

Then told me, "Closer."

This was her room, her house, and she was in charge!

She asked for my hand, took it in hers, peered with absolute focus into my eyes, and started asking all about me. She wanted to learn about my work, about my faith life, and about my family.

I soon realized that this woman may have been in that bed for the last six years, but she was just as much alive, active, and present as my kids were on that train.

She was doing pretty darn good for being 105 years old!

We had an amazing visit. As I prepared to leave, she told it to me straight: "John"—her blue eyes glistened—"listen to me, you need to wake up. Your family needs you to lead them. It's time to wake up now. No more living idly. No more excuses. No more sleepwalking. It's time to wake up!"

She didn't say pray daily (though that's something I aim to do).

She didn't promise miracles (though I know they are always coming).

She put my fate straight into my own hands.

Time to wake up.

The simple mantra of a remarkable woman.

Every time I see the picture of Sister Gertrude I'm reminded of her zest, courage, and faithfulness. It also reminds me of many others who offered the same advice to me.

After all, what did my brother Jim say to me the day I was burned as I lay shivering in shock in the cold St. Louis snow? "John, wake up! Stay awake! You can't go to sleep!"

What did Jack Buck say to me every time he came into my hospital room?

"Kid, wake up!"

Throughout my career as a student, I always had teachers yelling, "O'Leary, wake up!" (I tended to daydream in class.)

Every great spiritual teacher discusses the importance of being fully awake; of learning to live in the present moment. Not fixated on when things might get good in the future. Not mired in regret or defeat from something that happened in the past. But here. In this moment. In today.

The name Buddha means "awakened" or "I am awake." The center of my own faith, Jesus, often extolled his followers to wake up, to keep watch, to be alert, to be on the ready. Some of the last words Jesus spoke in the Garden of Gethsemane centered around staying awake.

This choice to be fully awake is just as important as all the other lessons included in this book. In fact, none of the seven choices matter if you haven't fully opened your eyes. None of the choices are even visible unless you actively seek the moment-by-moment inflection points, knowing that this instant, right now, is the most important in your life.

Every day holds the potential of a miracle.

Every moment, the seemingly positive or negative, provides the opportunity for possibility and beauty.

But you've got to open your eyes to see it. You've got to wake up.

A SECOND CHANCE

Beth and I ran to the car.

We jumped in as quickly as we could.

I turned the ignition, backed out of the garage, and raced to get there.

Just moments before we were sleeping. It was early on a Sunday morning and we woke up to the phone ringing. I struggled through the haze of my sleepiness to find the receiver.

"Hello?"

I heard my mom's voice.

It was distressed and hushed.

I listened, lost my breath, and responded.

I'll be right there.

Beth and I drove in silence.

Neither of us really knew what to say.

It didn't take long to get there.

I turned onto their street.

It's a drive I had made a million times. Home from school and church and dinners out. Home from friends' houses and family parties. Home after a five-month stint in the hospital.

I knew it well.

I loved it.

This time was different.

This time I dreaded it.

As we neared the house, my concern intensified.

Even before the house came into view, I could see smoke in the distance.

Yellow police tape blocked any access closer.

Several large red fire trucks idled in front of the house. Hoses were connected to fire hydrants.

These efforts were focused on my parents' house.

It was on fire.

Again.

How could this be happening?

What were the odds?

I couldn't believe it.

I parked the car, got out, and stared.

My heart sank watching thick smoke cascade from our house. I almost got sick watching firefighters break windows, flames leap from the roof line, and smoke rise to the heavens.

Over on a little hill to the side of the house, sitting beneath an oak tree, were Mom and Dad. Their arms around one another. Watching their home burn.

Again.

They'd been doing yard work that morning.

One of them put something in the toaster, went outside to get a little more work in, and it must have become lodged in the toaster. It caught on fire. The flames leaped to the wallpaper, ignited a cabinet, and spread through the kitchen. By the time my parents heard the house's fire alarm and saw the smoke, it was so intense that they weren't even able to get into the house.

By the time they woke a neighbor, called 911, and the firefighters arrived, it was too late. My parents' house was completely aflame.

Yes, they were safe.

No one was injured.

We were all grateful for that.

But this was painful.

This stung.

This burned.

As we sat on that hill together, tearful, watching our home burn, we began discussing what we'd do next.

They'd have to find a new place to stay. They'd need new clothes, they'd need new medicine for my dad, toiletries for my mom. They'd need to rebuild their life. And they'd have to rebuild their house.

Then I hugged them both and spoke.

Don't worry. It will all be okay.

And I said it with confidence.

Years earlier many people had scoffed at my choice to become a contractor.

Why would a guy without fingers, who doesn't do well in the heat, with a college degree in finance, go into a business where his scarred skin would take a beating, where he'd sweat like crazy all day long, and where he'd come home exhausted each night . . . only to wake up early and do it again?

Sometimes I questioned the choice myself.

But deep down I knew why I chose it.

Ever since the fire, I'd worked hard to overcome possible limitations and prove to people that I could do anything. I certainly could've chosen a desk job. Instead I chose to hammer nails, climb ladders, do the physical stuff I think people assumed I couldn't do.

But as I stood there, watching my childhood home in flames again, I felt I finally understood that there was a purpose to all of it.

Being a contractor, I finally had something truly worthy to build.

Being a contractor, I could rebuild the same home I burned down two decades earlier.

Being a contractor, I could shoulder much of the stress, sadness, and burden that would otherwise confront my parents.

Being a contractor, I could provide this small gift to my parents.

Mom and Dad had given me my life, loved me as a child, helped me rebuild after my fire, and supported and encouraged me mightily in the years since.

In other words, they loved me.

I now had an opportunity to reflect a little of their love back to them.

Later that day as the fire trucks pulled out, we waded back into our home. The house was darkened and charred. The terrible odor of burned debris made breathing difficult. We picked through the remnants of the house. We still had a few photo albums. We still had our family and friends. We still had a strong faith that God works through all things. And we still knew, absolutely *knew*, that in spite of these ashes the best was yet to come.

We knew that we could rebuild.

We knew it would be okay.

And we knew the truth behind the words Marshal Ferdinand Foch wrote a century earlier: "The most powerful weapon on earth is the human soul on fire."

WHAT DOES IT MEAN TO ME?

It was my first speaking trip out of the country.

I was nervous and unsure of myself.

I still wasn't certain how to tell my story or what it meant to the audience. I needed *them* to approve of *me*. That's the wrong attitude to have in life, and certainly the wrong attitude as a speaker.

During the question-and-answer portion, a gentleman near the back of the room stood. He was handed a microphone. He began his question by thanking me for the time, for the story, for the courage. Then he said, "But . . ."

Ah, I hate that word! It deletes and invalidates everything that was spoken before it!

"But, what does any of it have to do with me?"

He had a good point!

My friend, at this point in the book I expect you are able to answer that for yourselves. I hope that you understand the immense power in your choices. I pray that you now understand that your life is a beautiful story.

But you've got to have the eyes to see it.

It may not be exactly like the story you'd dreamed for your life, but it is perfectly yours. And what comes next is completely up to you.

Perhaps it's time to stop wishing you were someone else. Maybe now is the time to wake up to the beauty of your life today.

Were things perfect when Gino walked in, victorious, and on fire after scoring that goal?

Of course not! I was lying face freaking down in the bed! My entire body was an open wound and I was in incredible pain.

But I could still see the opportunity to party!

Things may not be perfect in your life.

They rarely are.

The key, then, is to choose to dance through the imperfection, through the pain and splints, and even as you're strapped down to the bed.

You see, we can't wait for the perfect circumstances to join the party. It's time to wake up and participate now. Because every moment matters. Every day counts. Every minute is an opportunity.

I hope you see that my story is a testament that no matter what adversity comes your way, it's not the end of the story. If you can learn to see it as an opportunity to overcome, to learn, to stretch, to wake up, to ask, *Where might this be leading me?*— you'll realize the strength you have within. And it is more than enough.

There is a quote that I love. Some attribute it to John Lennon. "Everything will be all right in the end. So if it is not all right, it is not yet the end."

If it is not all right . . . it is not yet the end.

That, you see, is faith.

If people see the snapshot of me in that hospital bed that first night after the fire, they assume that my life is a tragedy. But fast-forward twenty years later and they'd see me standing up at the altar, waiting for a beautiful woman, the love of my life, to walk down the aisle.

"If everything is not yet all right, it is not yet the end."

If people saw a snapshot of me speaking to four Girl Scouts, behind a desk, staring at a piece of paper, overwhelmed by the moment, they'd assume it's time for the poor fella to find new work. But fast-forward ten years and they'd see a photo of me speaking in front of thousands of people.

"If everything is not yet all right, it is not yet the end."

And if people saw a snapshot of me swinging a hammer, wedged awkwardly between two hands with no fingers, they'd likely think this kid should consider a different path. But fast-forward to shortly after my parents' second fire and they'd see a determined leader orchestrating the rapid rebuilding of a burned-out house.

"If everything is not yet all right, it is not yet the end."

You see, there is always a chance for redemption.

There is always a chance to rebuild.

There is always a miracle just waiting around the corner.

But you've got to open your eyes to see it.

This book is your invitation to start living your life again.

You now have the information.

You know you have the power.

You can choose to hit snooze again; to keep sleepwalking in zombie land.

But don't confuse being out of bed with being awake.

Don't confuse being superbusy with being actually effective.

And don't confuse not being dead with being fully alive.

This is your chance. You can hop out of bed, see the inflection point before you, and own your decision of which way to move forward.

You can see your life for the adventure it is.

You can set your life ablaze.

You can lead a radically inspired life.

And it all starts now.

This is your time.

This is your day.

Live inspired.

ACKNOWLEDGMENTS

"I alone cannot change the world. But I can cast a stone across the waters to create many ripples."
—*Mother Teresa*

Sometimes we don't take action, stretch ourselves, or take risks because we don't think one phone call, one conversation, or one person can make a difference.

We don't believe that we can, in fact, change our own world, let alone the entire world.

After reading *On Fire*, you know that one of the greatest heroes of my life is Hall of Fame announcer Jack Buck.

His life undoubtedly changed mine.

But don't forget how Jack Buck knew to visit me.

A friend of my family, Colleen Schoendienst, called to tell her dad, Red, about the fire. She asked if he would keep me in his prayers. That night her dad went to a charity event and sat next to his friend Jack Buck. He mentioned the phone call he'd had with his daughter.

The following day Jack visited me. The darkness and pain were replaced with light and possibility.

My life changed.

One phone call. One mention. One visit.

There is simply no doubt that more than one person changed my life. It's just impossible to appropriately thank them all.

So, thank you to all of the Colleens and the Reds and the Jacks. To the classmates, coworkers, and friends. Each of you, each of us, do in fact change the world.

I would be remiss not to acknowledge my amazing family. My parents, Susan and Denny, and my siblings Jim, Cadey, Amy, Susan, and Laura: you are the ones who gave me life. You are the ones who saved my life. You are the ones who filled my earliest memories with joy, faith, and laughter. And you are the ones who continue to encourage and love me today.

My beautiful wife, Beth. You bring more joy to my days than I knew possible. I am so blessed to know you, love you, and raise our kids with you. I fall more in love with you every day. And my kids, Jack, Patrick, Henry, and Grace: you make your mother and me proud, happy, and love-filled beyond words.

And finally, my writing team. Whew! *On Fire* had been a dream of mine for years. Without this all-star team, it would not have been possible. I am eternally grateful for your guidance.

Michael Palgon, my New York, no-bull agent. You worked tirelessly for three years, pushing this Midwestern kid to dig deep to "find the story." Your laser focus on keeping my authentic voice, impacting each reader, and navigating the publishing world was invaluable. Thank you.

Cindy DiTiberio, my editor and copilot. Writing a book can be an exhausting, lonely process. Having you as a copilot as we worked through challenges, uncovered important stories, discovered the arc of the book, and journeyed together was a joy. *On Fire* would simply not be without your efforts.

The brilliant Michele Martin, my publisher; my incredibly dedicated editor, Michelle Howry; and the entire North Star Way team at Simon & Schuster. Your belief in *On Fire* and its potential to touch readers from day one is what fueled me to see this project through. Thank you for your unwavering support, extraordinary vision, and passion for the work that you do.

I not only have the best job in the world, but also the best team making it a reality. So a massive thank you to my tremendously passionate team at JohnOlearyInspires.com including Deanna McClintock Lester, Abby Richter, Molly Frank, and Sandy Montgomery. Because of you and our mentors, clients, partners, and board members with whom we've had the honor of working, it is possible for me to empower others to live inspired. Through sharing your wisdom, support, and time, you have touched countless lives—including mine.

And finally to you, the reader. It was my hope when I began writing this book that I would be able to share the lessons that most dramatically and positively impacted me and encouraged me to live a radically inspired life every day. This is your invitation to ignite *your* radically inspired life.

May you realize the impact of your life and may you live inspired.

MY *ON FIRE* JOURNEY

The O'Learys taking a family picture in spring of 1980. From left to right: Jim, Amy, Susan, John, little Susan, Denny, and Cadey.

LEFT: The gas can that exploded on January 17, 1987. RIGHT: The resulting damage in the O'Leary family garage after the fire.

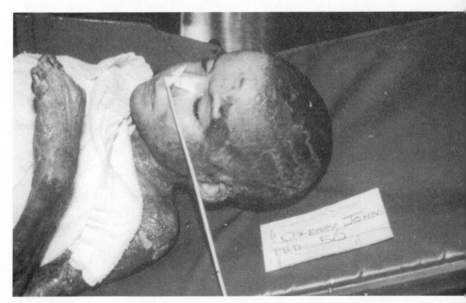

John shortly after the fire, burned on 100 percent of his body and not expected to survive.

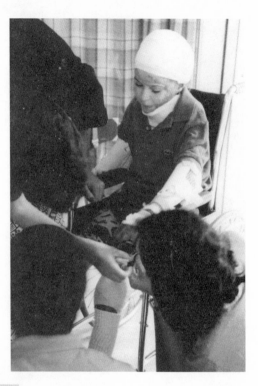

John receiving in-patient physical therapy.

John and his older brother Jim, who saved his life, on a family vacation in the mountains the summer after the fire.

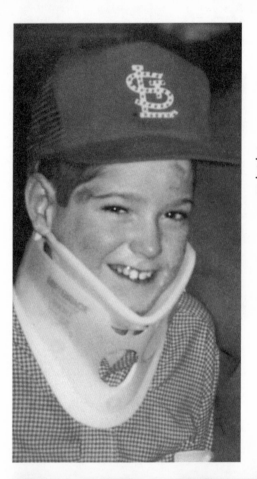

John smiles broadly, celebrating John O'Leary Day at Busch Stadium.

Jack Buck encouraged John to learn how to write again by sending him baseballs signed by St. Louis Cardinals players.

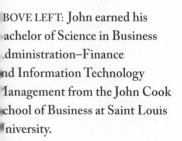

BOVE LEFT: John earned his
achelor of Science in Business
dministration–Finance
nd Information Technology
lanagement from the John Cook
chool of Business at Saint Louis
niversity.

BOVE RIGHT: Jack Buck came to
hn's college graduation.

IGHT: Jack Buck gave his MLB
all of Fame Crystal Baseball to
hn as a gift when he graduated
om Saint Louis University.

John married Beth Hittler on November 22, 2003.

John, Jim, Susan, Denny, Laura, Cadey, Amy, and Susan O'Leary on vacation together with their families in Florida, summer 2015.

A client of John's, Alabama Power, reunited "Nurse Roy" and John in 2011.

John speaks to more than 50,000 people each year.

John with his wife, Beth, and children Jack, Patrick, Henry, and Grace O'Leary in 2014.

ABOUT THE AUTHOR

Expected to die, John O'Leary now teaches others how to truly live.

In 1987, John O'Leary was a curious nine-year-old boy. Playing with fire and gasoline, John created a massive explosion in his home and was burned on 100 percent of his body. He was given less than a 1 percent chance to live.

Enduring five months in the hospital and years in therapy, John not only survived, but thrived. He learned to walk and write again. He went back to grade school, graduated high school and then college. He started his own real estate development business, became a chaplain at a children's hospital, and is an international inspirational speaker.

This epic story of survival remained untold for almost two decades until it was first showcased in his parents' book, *Overwhelming Odds*, in 2004. Originally printing 200 copies for friends and family, his parents have sold more than 70,000 copies. That book finally freed John to embrace his miraculous recovery and share it with the world.

As a speaker, John shares his message each year with more than 50,000 people at more than 120 events held by organizations in healthcare, sales, marketing, financial services, education, spirituality, and safety. Some of John's clients include Southwest Airlines, LEGO, Enterprise Rent-A-Car, and many more. His emotional storytelling, unexpected humor, and authenticity make each of his presentations truly transformational.

John has an online community of more than 70,000 and is a contributing writer to several publications, including *The Huffington Post* and ParadeMagazine.com. In addition to writing and speaking, he actively invests his time serving in his church, community, and various charitable organizations.

Residing in his hometown of St. Louis, Missouri, he considers his greatest successes to be his marriage to his wife, Beth, and their four children, Jack, Patrick, Henry, and Grace. They inspire him to make as great a difference as possible through his work each day—and to race home afterward to spend as much time with them as possible.

The boy that was expected to die now enjoys a radically inspired life. He invites you to learn more and continue your journey online at www.JohnOLearyInspires.com.